PIANO · VOCAL · GUITAR

PAUL McCARTNEY   OUT THERE

ISBN 978-1-4803-9098-0

MPL COMMUNICATIONS, INC.
http://www.mplcommunications.com
EXCLUSIVELY DISTRIBUTED BY

HAL•LEONARD®
CORPORATION
7777 W. BLUEMOUND RD. P.O. BOX 13819 MILWAUKEE, WI 53213

Visit Hal Leonard Online at
www.halleonard.com

SET LIST

Paul McCartney OUT THERE tour

Eight Days a Week
Junior's Farm
All My Loving
Listen to What the Man Said
Let Me Roll It
Paperback Writer
My Valentine
Nineteen Hundred and Eighty Five
The Long and Winding Road
Maybe I'm Amazed
I've Just Seen a Face
We Can Work It Out
Another Day
And I Love Her
Blackbird
Here Today
Your Mother Should Know
Lady Madonna
All Together Now
Mrs. Vandebilt
Eleanor Rigby
Lovely Rita
Being for the Benefit of Mr. Kite!
Something
Ob-La-Di, Ob-La-Da
Band on the Run
Back in the U.S.S.R.
Let It Be
Live and Let Die
Hey Jude
Hi, Hi, Hi

Encore:

Day Tripper
I Saw Her Standing There
Get Back

Encore 2:

Yesterday
Helter Skelter
Golden Slumbers
Carry That Weight
The End

CONTENTS

4	All My Loving
7	All Together Now
12	And I Love Her
16	Another Day
22	Back in the U.S.S.R.
26	Band on the Run
31	Being for the Benefit of Mr. Kite!
36	Blackbird
40	Carry That Weight
46	Day Tripper
50	Eight Days a Week
43	Eleanor Rigby
54	The End
59	Get Back
62	Golden Slumbers
65	Helter Skelter
72	Here Today
82	Hey Jude
77	Hi, Hi, Hi
86	I Saw Her Standing There
92	I've Just Seen a Face
96	Junior's Farm
106	Lady Madonna
101	Let It Be
110	Let Me Roll It
112	Listen to What the Man Said
116	Live and Let Die
120	The Long and Winding Road
124	Lovely Rita
129	Maybe I'm Amazed
132	Mrs. Vandebilt
140	My Valentine
144	Nineteen Hundred and Eighty Five
154	Ob-La-Di, Ob-La-Da
160	Paperback Writer
151	Something
164	We Can Work It Out
167	Yesterday
170	Your Mother Should Know

ALL MY LOVING

Words and Music by JOHN LENNON
and PAUL McCARTNEY

D.S. al Coda
(Verse 1)
(take 2nd ending)

CODA

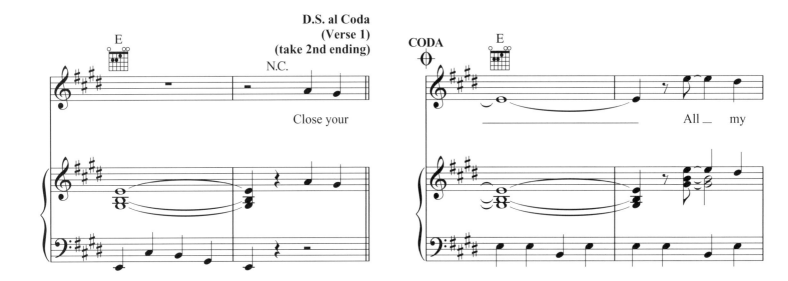

Close your

All __ my

lov - ing, _____ all __ my lov - ing, _____ ooh, ___ all __ my

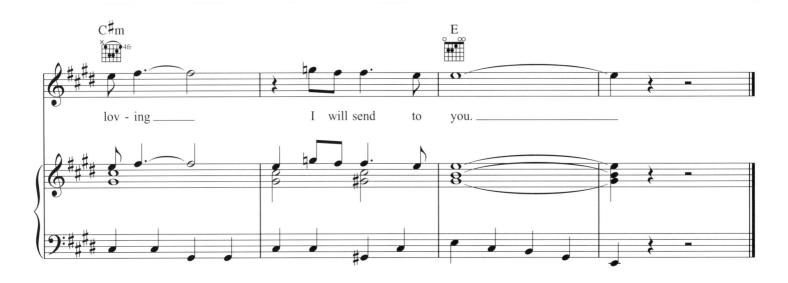

lov - ing _____ I will send to you. _____

ALL TOGETHER NOW

Words and Music by JOHN LENNON
and PAUL McCARTNEY

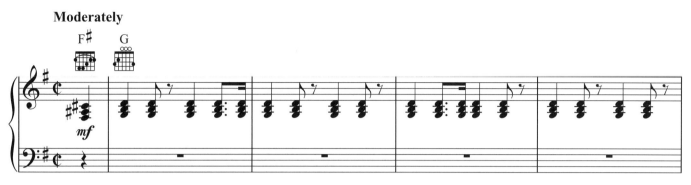

One, two, three, four, can I have __ a lit-tle more? __

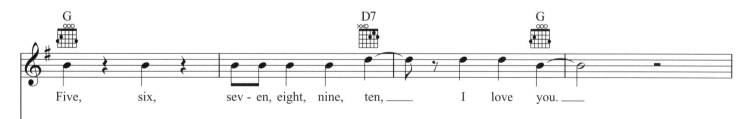

Five, six, sev-en, eight, nine, ten, ___ I love you. ___

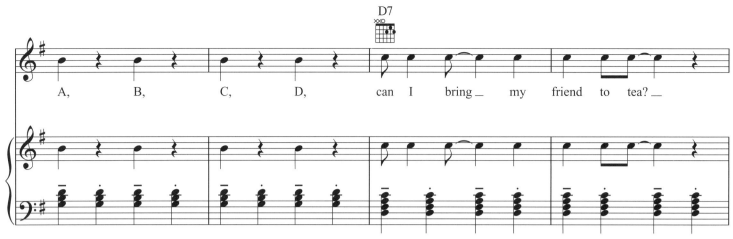

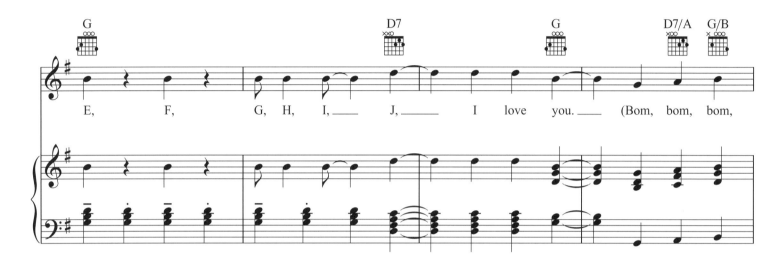

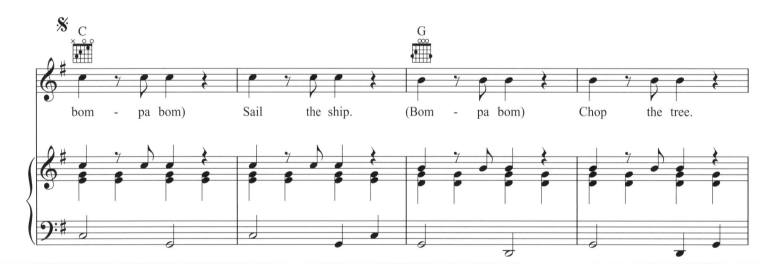

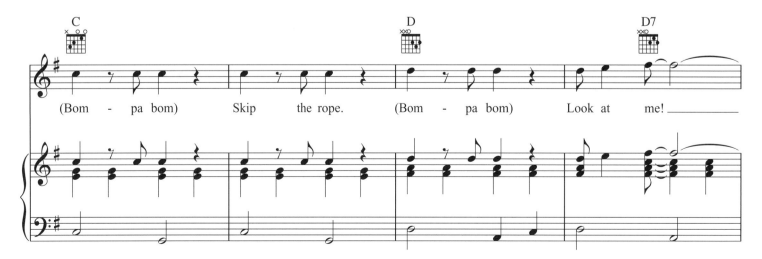

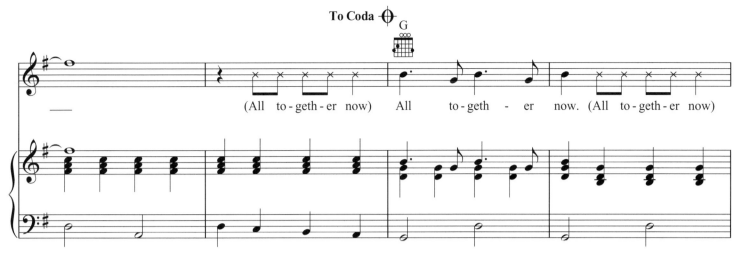

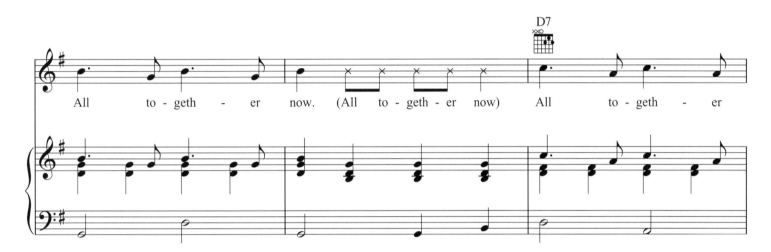

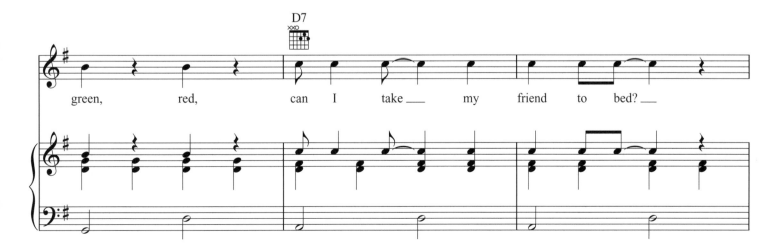

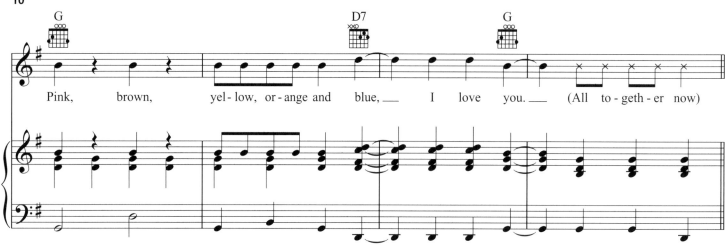

Pink, brown, yel-low, or-ange and blue, __ I love you. __ (All to-geth-er now)

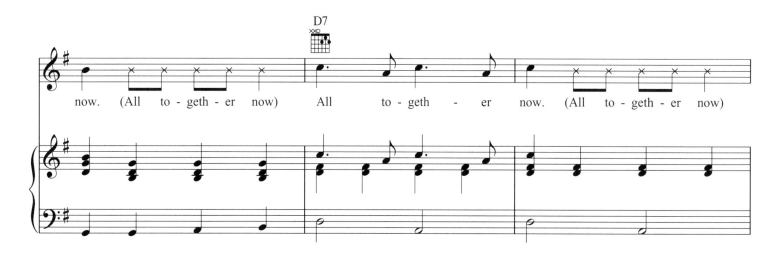

All to-geth - er now. (All to-geth-er now) All to-geth - er

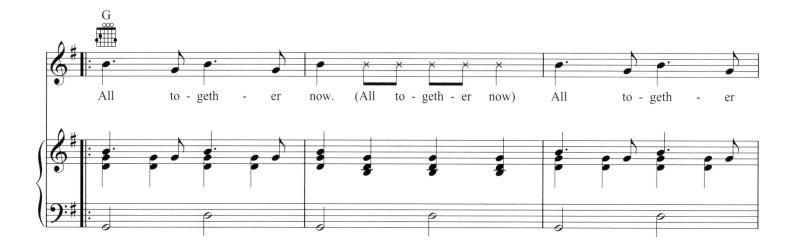

now. (All to-geth-er now) All to-geth - er now. (All to-geth-er now)

All to-geth - er now. (All to-geth-er now) now. (Bom, bom, bom,

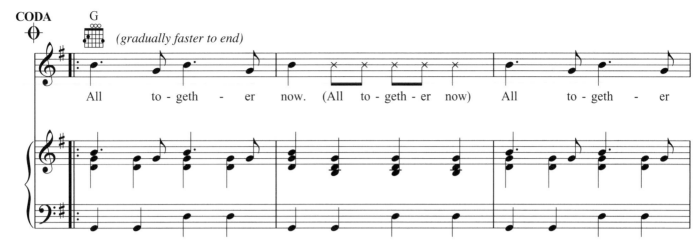

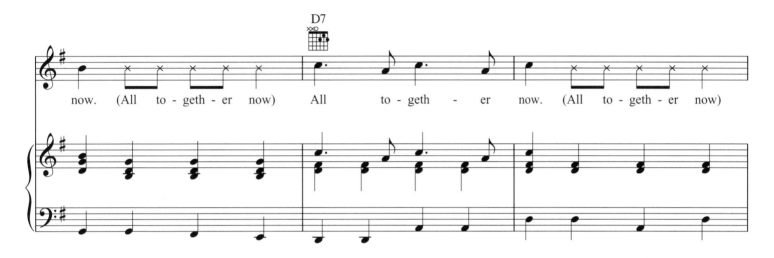

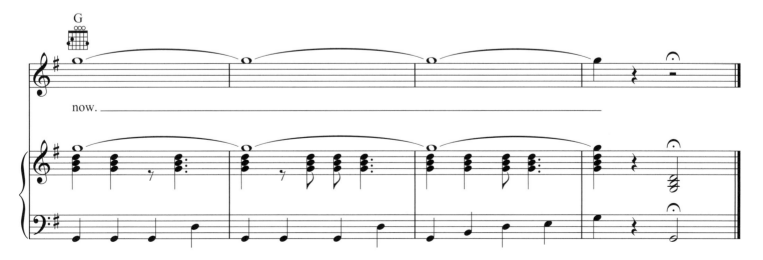

AND I LOVE HER

Words and Music by JOHN LENNON
and PAUL McCARTNEY

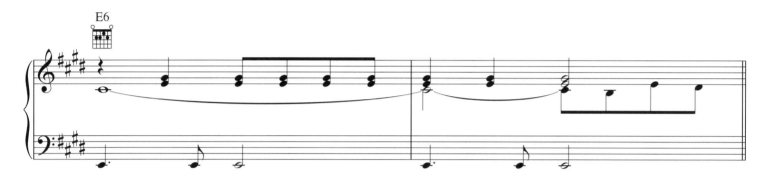

I give her all my love,
She gives me ev-'ry-thing
Bright are the stars that shine,

that's all I do.
and ten-der-ly.
dark is the sky.

And if you saw ___ my love, ___ you'd love her too. ___
The kiss my lov - er brings ___ she brings to me. ___
I know this love ___ of mine ___ will nev - er die. ___

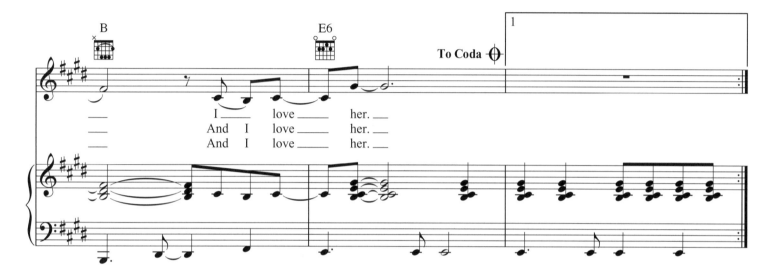

I ___ love ___ her. ___
And I love ___ her. ___
And I love ___ her. ___

A love like ours ___

could nev - er die ___ as long as I ___

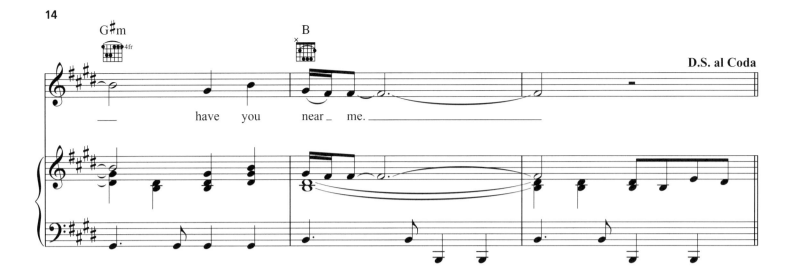

D.S. al Coda

have you near me.

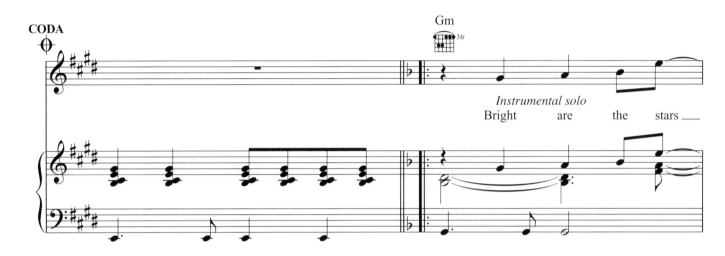

CODA

Instrumental solo
Bright are the stars

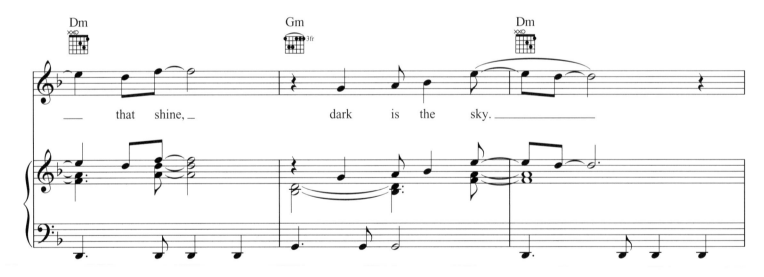

that shine, dark is the sky.

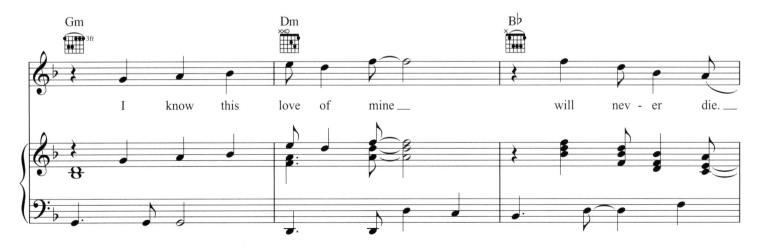

I know this love of mine will nev - er die.

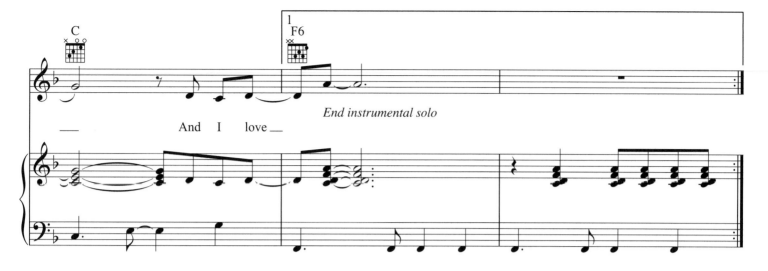

End instrumental solo

And I love ___

her. ___

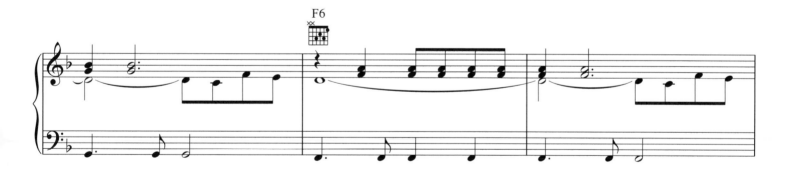

ANOTHER DAY

Words and Music by PAUL McCARTNEY
and LINDA McCARTNEY

Moderately

Ev - 'ry day she takes a morn - ing bath she wets her hair,

wraps a tow'l a - round her as she's head - ing for the bed - room chair, __ it's just an - oth - er day.

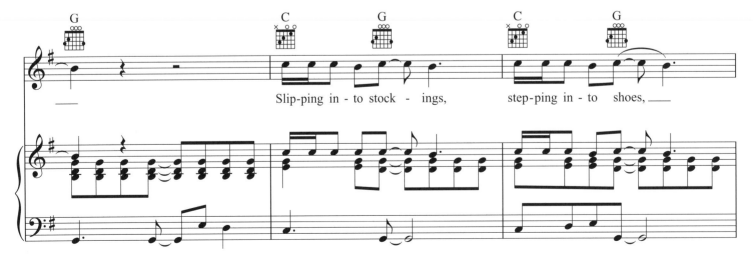

Slip - ping in - to stock - ings, step - ping in - to shoes, __

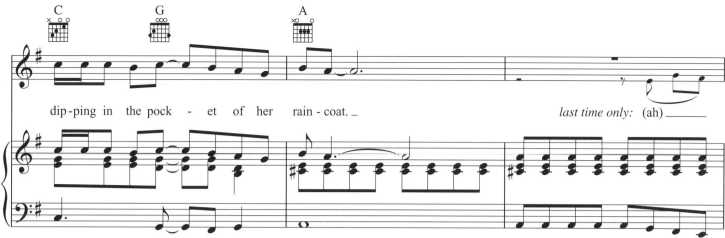

dip-ping in the pock - et of her rain-coat. _ *last time only:* (ah) _

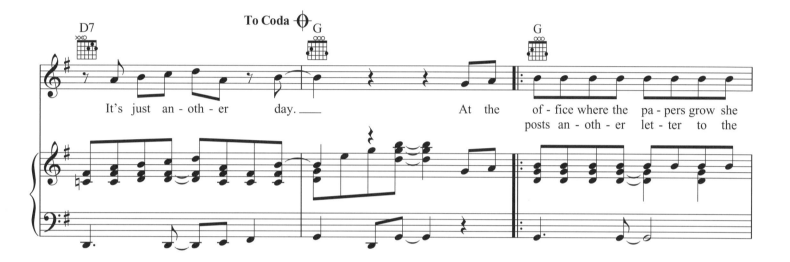

It's just an - oth - er day. _ At the of - fice where the pa - pers grow she
posts an - oth - er let - ter to the

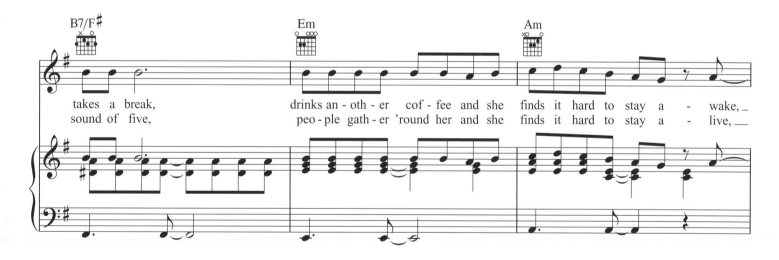

takes a break, drinks an - oth - er cof - fee and she finds it hard to stay a - wake, _
sound of five, peo - ple gath - er 'round her and she finds it hard to stay a - live, _

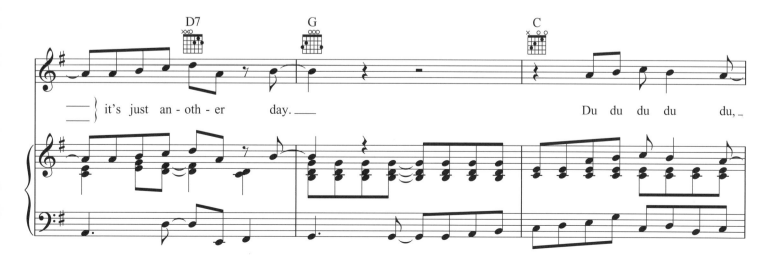

_ it's just an - oth - er day. _ Du du du du du, _

it's just an-oth-er day. ___ Du du du du du, ___ it's just an-oth-er day. ___

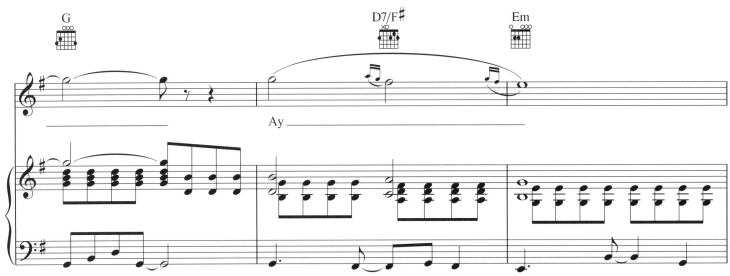

Ay ___

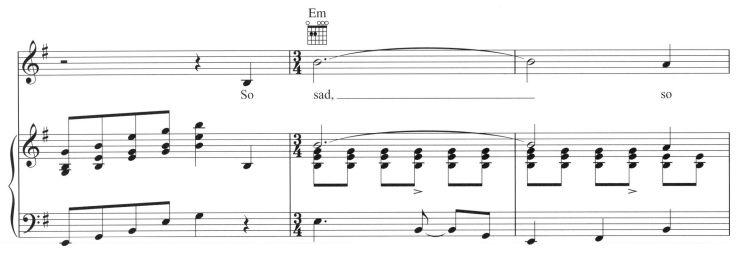

So sad, ___ so

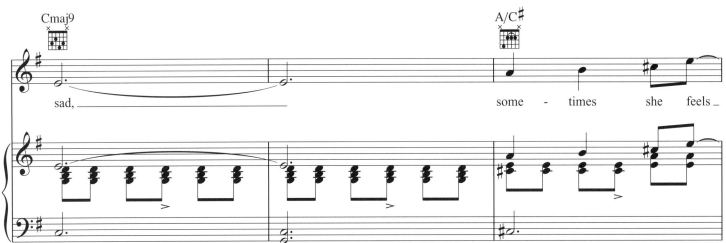

sad, ___ some-times she feels ___

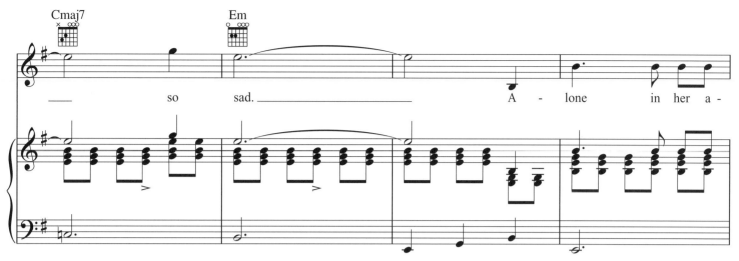

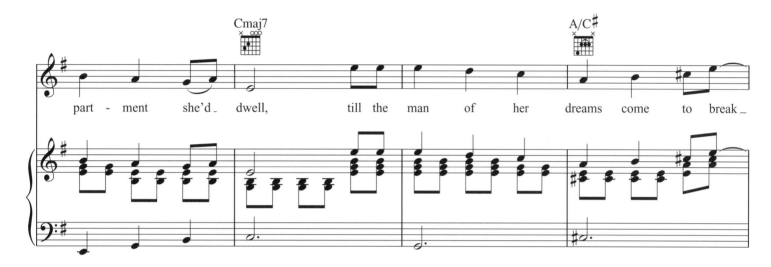

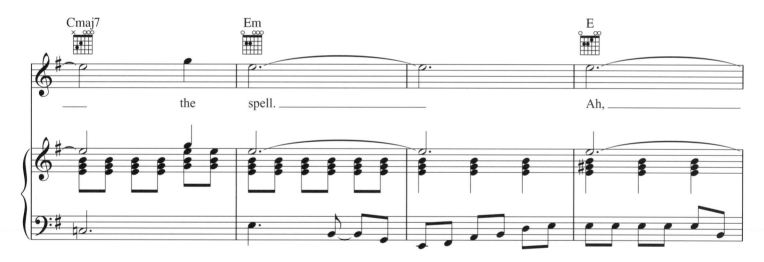

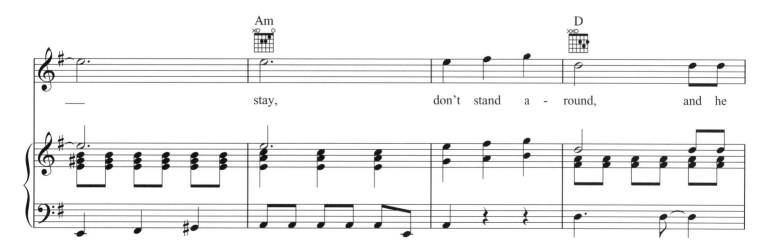

comes and he stays but he leaves the next

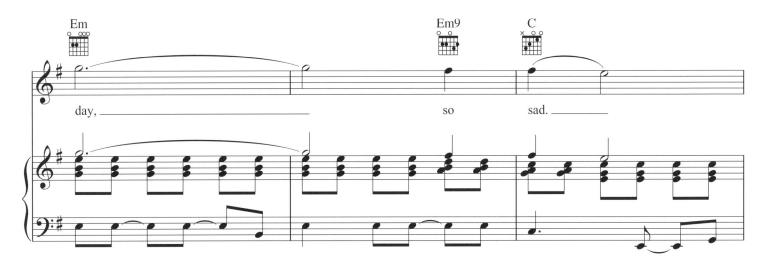

day, _____ so sad. _____

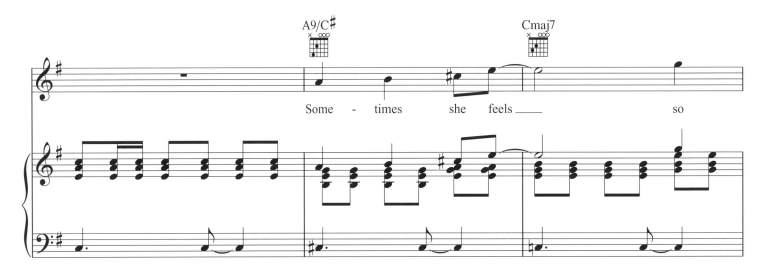

Some - times she feels _____ so

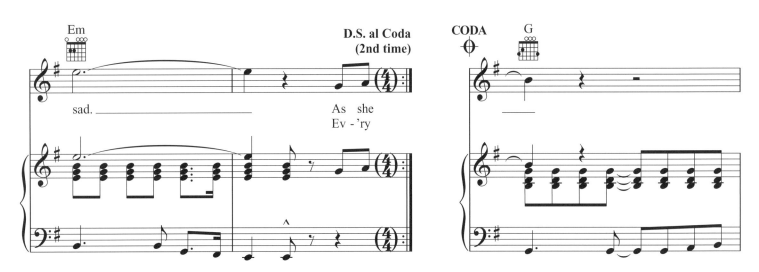

sad. _____ As she
Ev -'ry

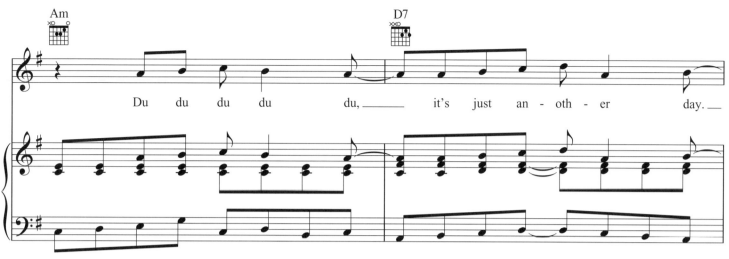

Du du du du du, _____ it's just an - oth - er day. ___

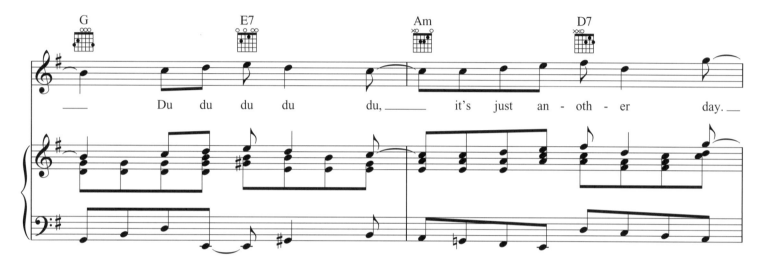

___ Du du du du du, _____ it's just an - oth - er day. ___

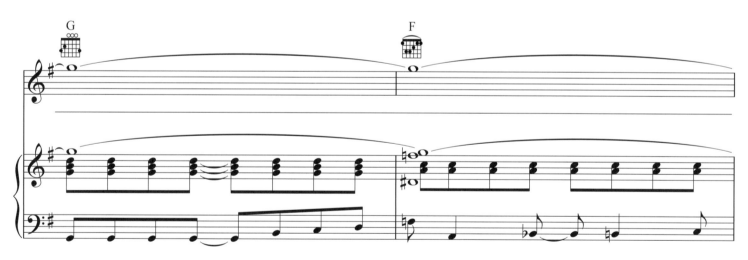

BACK IN THE U.S.S.R.

Words and Music by JOHN LENNON
and PAUL McCARTNEY

the way the pa - per bag was on my knee, ___ Man ___
it till to - mor - row to un - pack my case, ___ Hon -
me hear your bal - a - lai - kas ring - ing out, ___ Come ___

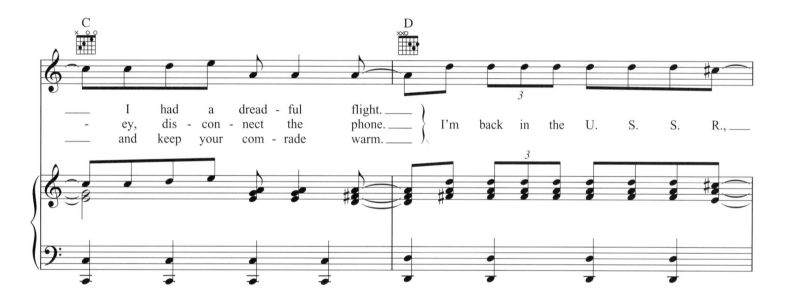

___ I had a dread - ful flight. ___
- ey, dis - con - nect the phone. ___ } I'm back in the U. S. S. R., ___
___ and keep your com - rade warm. ___

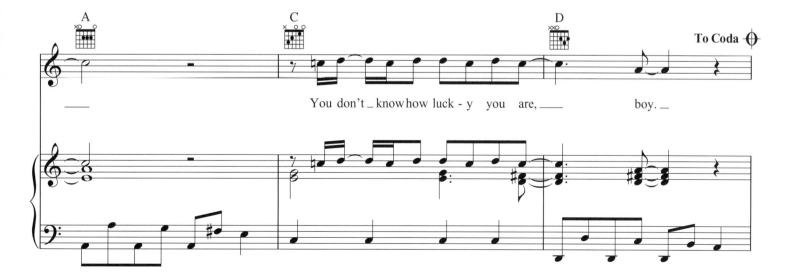

You don't ___ know how luck - y you are, ___ boy. ___

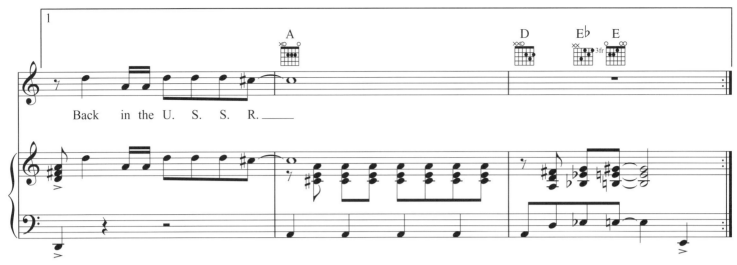

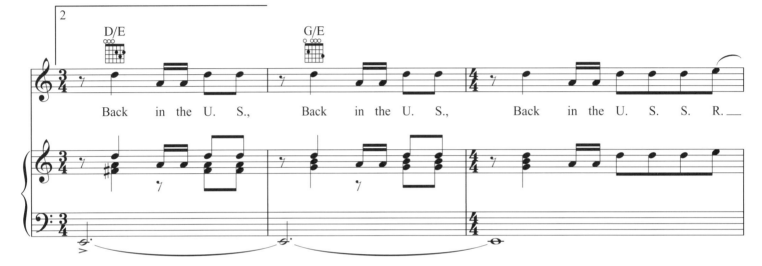

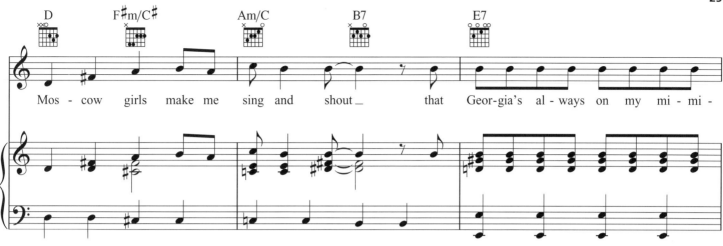

Mos - cow girls make me sing and shout __ that Geor-gia's al - ways on my mi - mi -

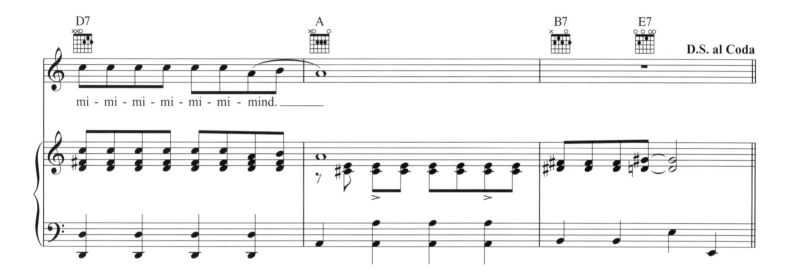

mi - mi - mi - mi - mi - mi - mi - mind. _____

D.S. al Coda

CODA

Back in the U. S. S. R. _____

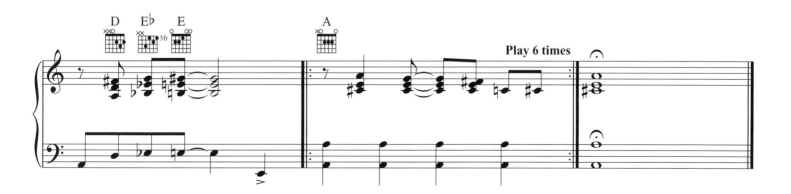

Play 6 times

BAND ON THE RUN

Words and Music by PAUL McCARTNEY
and LINDA McCARTNEY

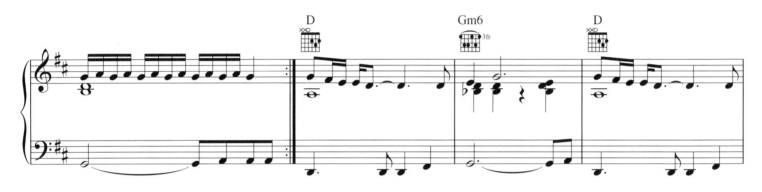

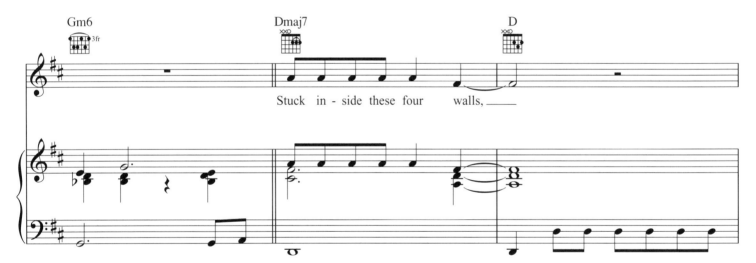

Stuck in-side these four walls, _____

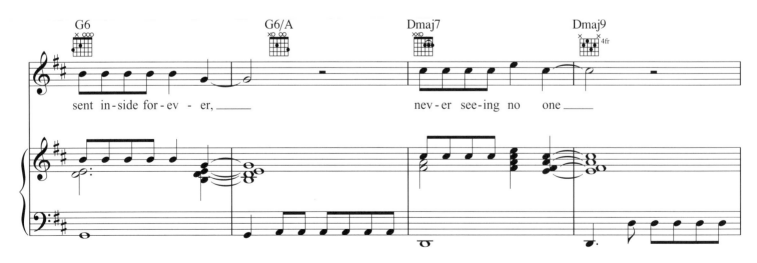

sent in-side for-ev-er, _____ nev-er see-ing no one _____

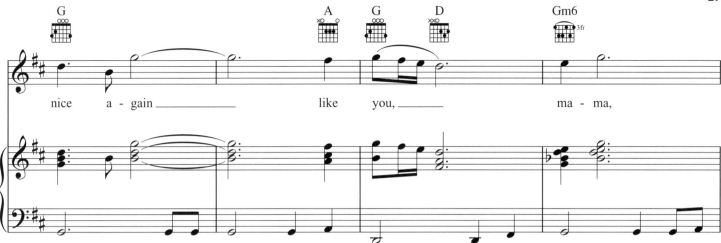

nice a - gain _____ like you, _____ ma - ma,

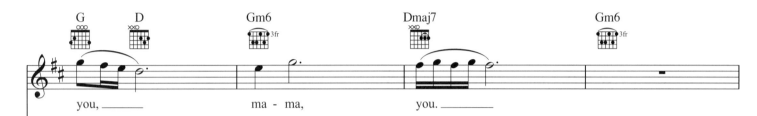

you, _____ ma - ma, you.

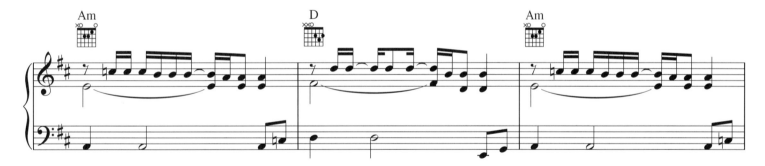

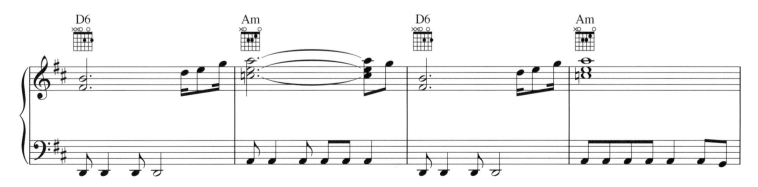

If I ev-er get out __ of here thought of giv-ing it all __ a-way to a reg-is-tered char - i - ty.

All I need is a pint __ a day if I ev-er get out __ of here, __ (if we ev-er get out __ of here.) __

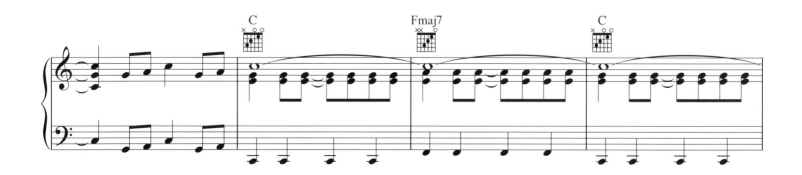

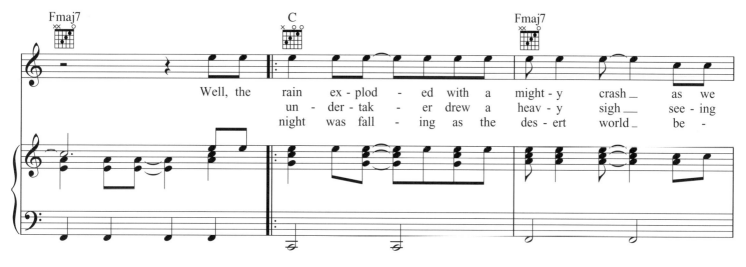

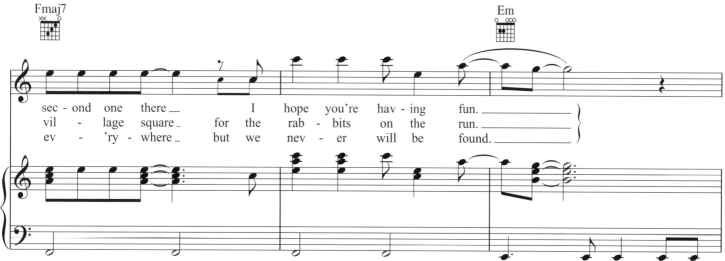

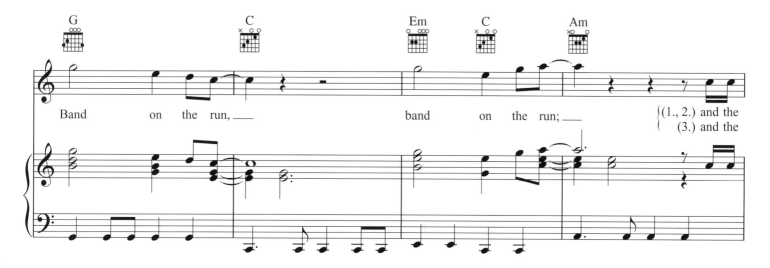

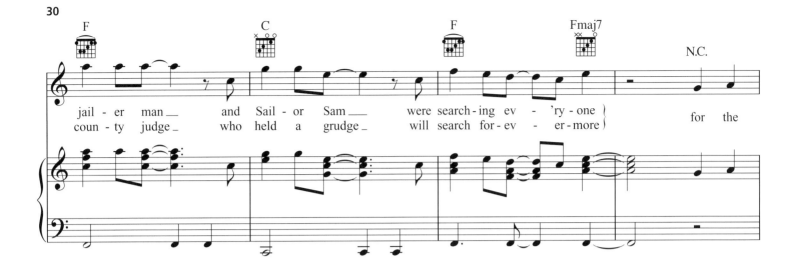

jail - er man ___ and Sail - or Sam ___ were search-ing ev - 'ry-one
coun - ty judge ___ who held a grudge ___ will search for-ev - er-more

for the

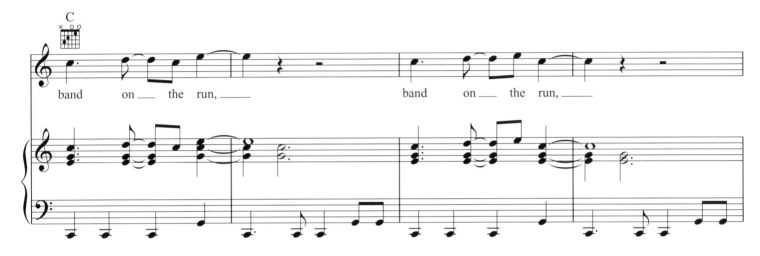

band on ___ the run, ___

band on ___ the run, ___

band on ___ the run, ___

band on ___ the run. ___

Well, the
Well, the

band on ___ the run. ___

BEING FOR THE BENEFIT OF MR. KITE!

Words and Music by JOHN LENNON
and PAUL McCARTNEY

ben-e-fit ___ of Mis-ter Kite, there will be ___ a show to-night on tram-po-line.
cel-e-brat-ed Mis-ter K., per-forms his feat ___ on Sat-ur-day at Bish-ops-gate.
band be-gins ___ at ten to six when Mis-ter K. ___ per-forms his tricks with-out a sound.

The Hen-der-sons will all be there, late of Pa-blo Fan-que's fair;
The Hen-der-sons will dance and sing as Mis-ter Kite flies through the ring;
And Mis-ter H. will dem-on-strate ten som-er-sets he'll un-der-take on

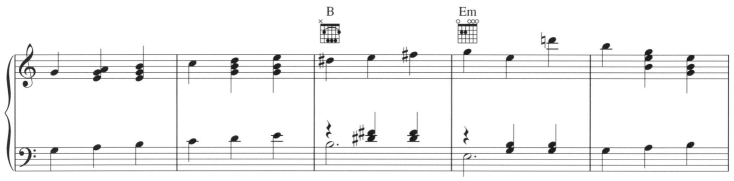

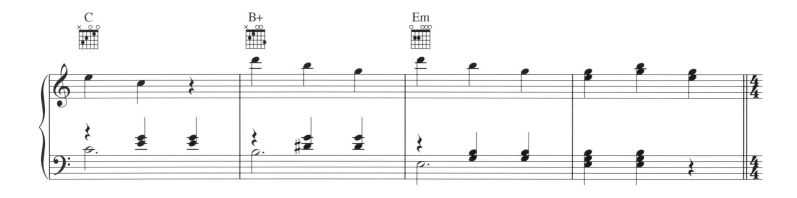

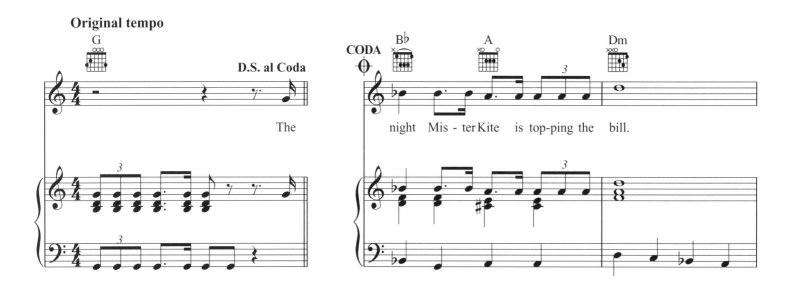

The night Mis - ter Kite is top-ping the bill.

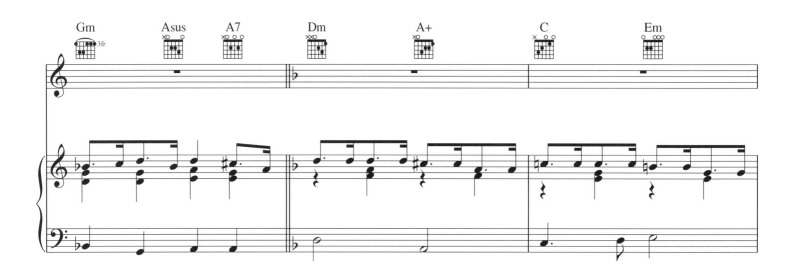

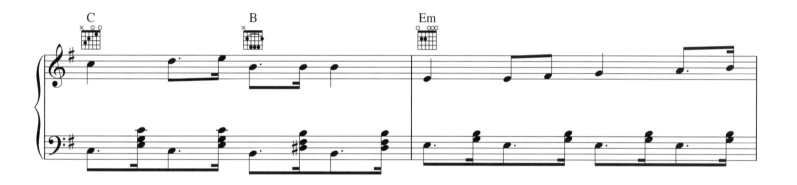

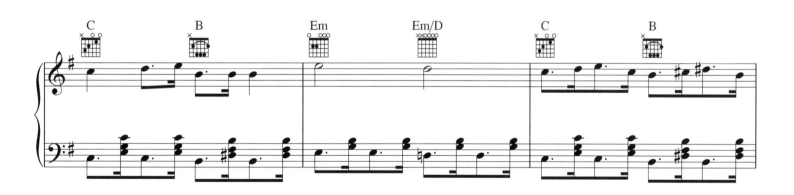

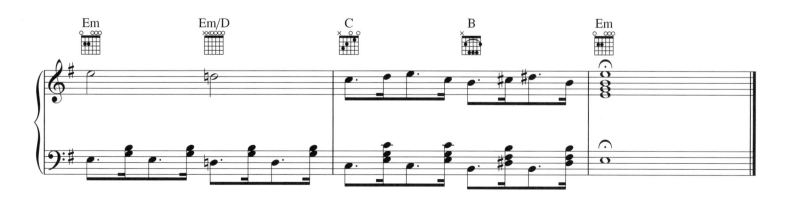

BLACKBIRD

Words and Music by JOHN LENNON
and PAUL McCARTNEY

Black-bird sing-ing in the dead of night,
Black-bird sing-ing in the dead of night,

take these bro-ken wings and learn to fly;
take these sunk-en eyes and learn to see;

all your life you were on-ly wait-ing for this mo-ment to a-
all your life you were on-ly wait-ing for this mo-ment to be

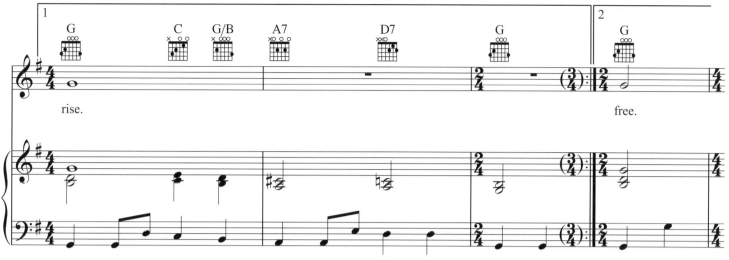

rise.   free.

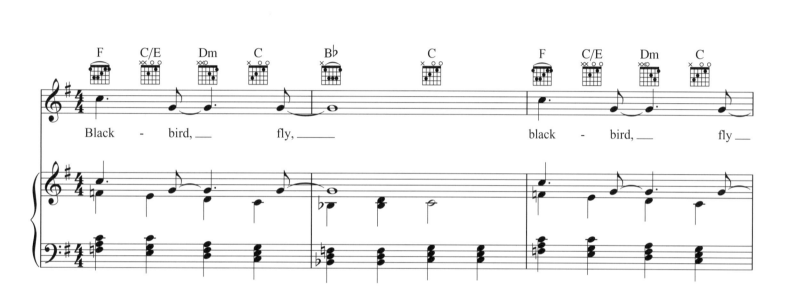

Black - bird, ___ fly, _____   black - bird, ___ fly ___

___   in - to the light of a dark black night. ____

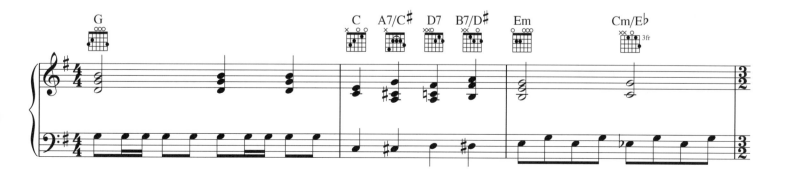

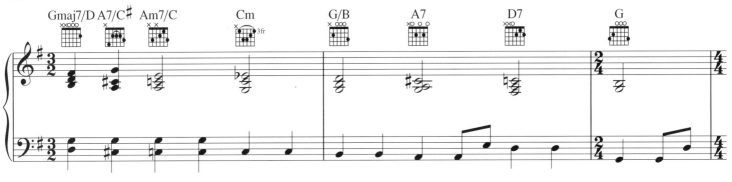

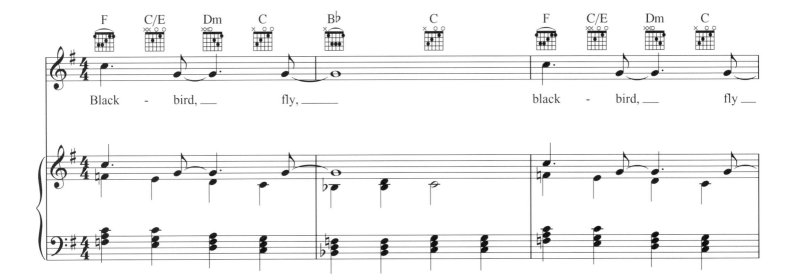

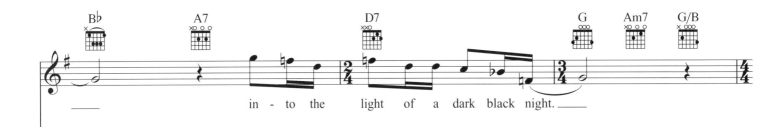

CARRY THAT WEIGHT

Words and Music by JOHN LENNON
and PAUL McCARTNEY

Boy, ____ you're gon-na car-ry that weight, __ car-ry that weight __ a long __

____ time. Boy, _____ you're gon-na car-ry that weight, __

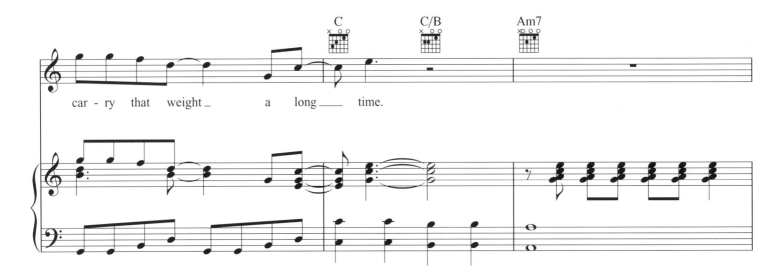

car-ry that weight __ a long ____ time.

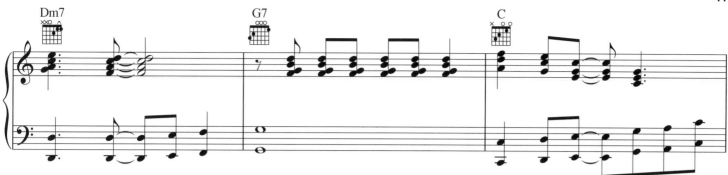

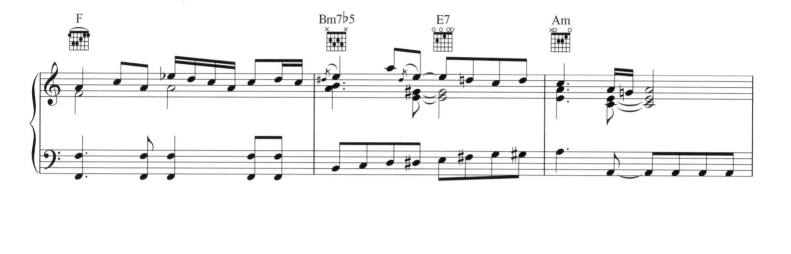

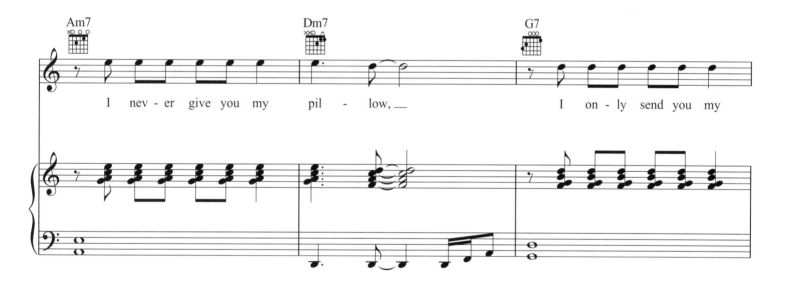

I nev-er give you my pil-low, ___ I on-ly send you my

in-vi-ta - tions. And in the mid-dle of the cel - e-bra - tions, I

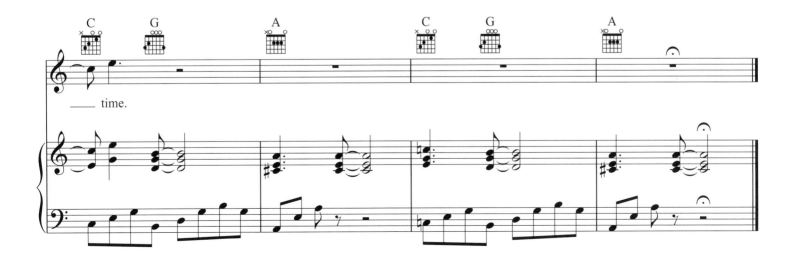

ELEANOR RIGBY

Words and Music by JOHN LENNON
and PAUL McCARTNEY

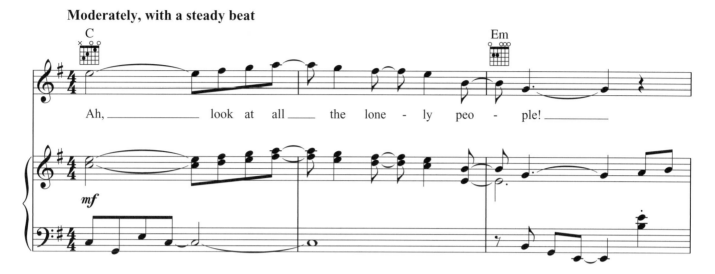

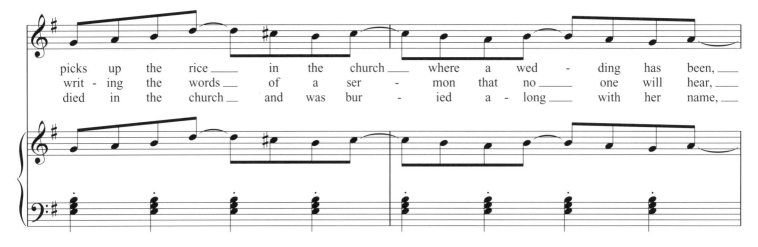

picks up the rice ___ in the church ___ where a wed - ding has been, ___
writ - ing the words ___ of a ser - mon that no ___ one will hear, ___
died in the church ___ and was bur - ied a - long ___ with her name, ___

C

Em

___ Lives in a dream. ___ Waits at the win - dow,
___ No one comes near. ___ Look at him work - ing,
___ No - bod - y came. ___ Fa - ther Mc - Ken - zie,

C

wear - ing the face ___ that she keeps ___ in a jar ___ by the door, ___
darn - ing his socks ___ in the night ___ when there's no - bod - y there, ___
wip - ing the dirt ___ from his hands ___ as he walks ___ from the grave, ___

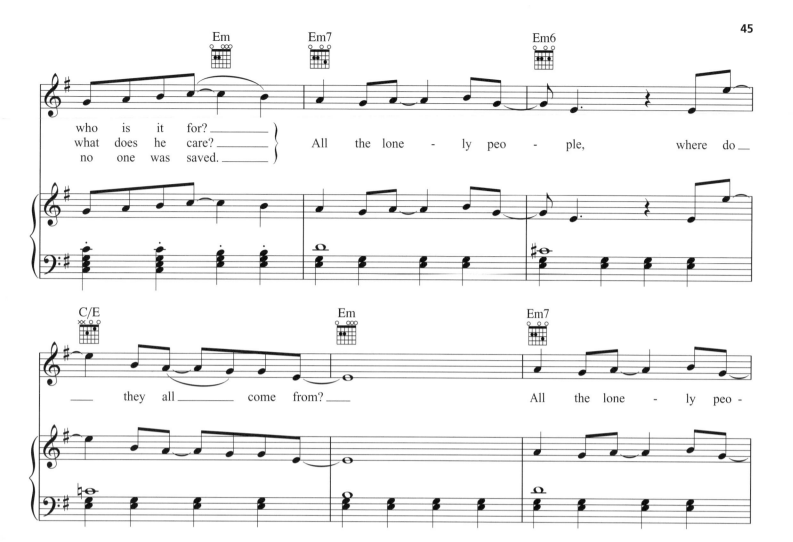

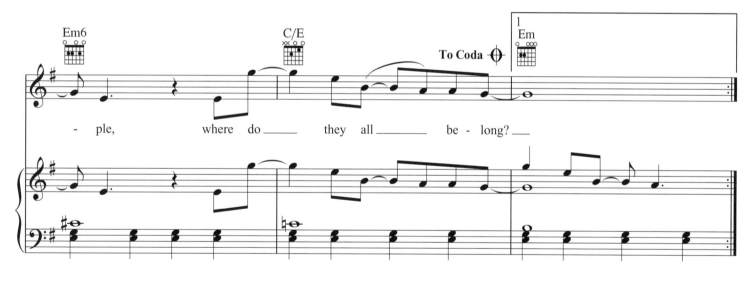

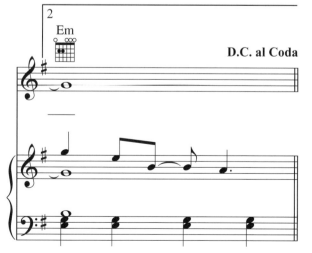

DAY TRIPPER

Words and Music by JOHN LENNON
and PAUL McCARTNEY

Moderate Rock

Got a good rea - son
She's a big teas - er,
Tried to please _ her,

for

It took me so _____ long _ to find out, _
It took me so _____ long _ to find out, _
It took me so _____ long _ to find out, _

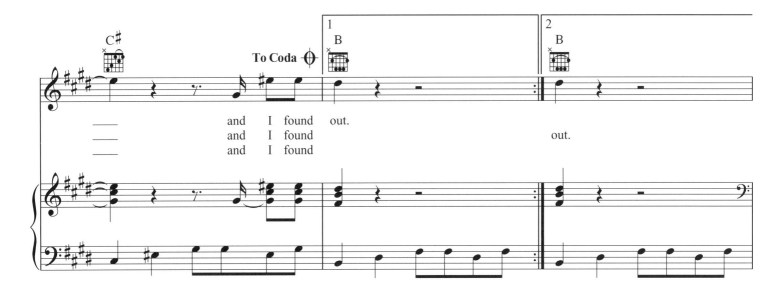

and I found out.
and I found out.
and I found

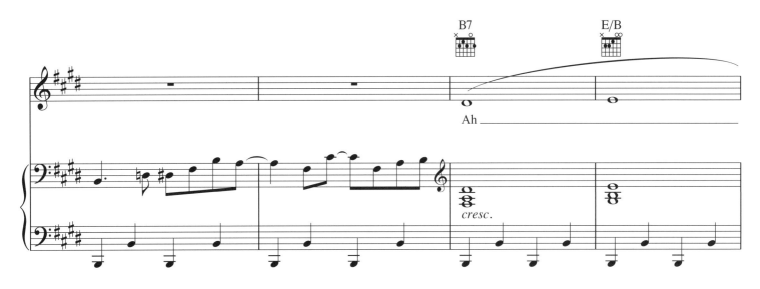

Ah _____

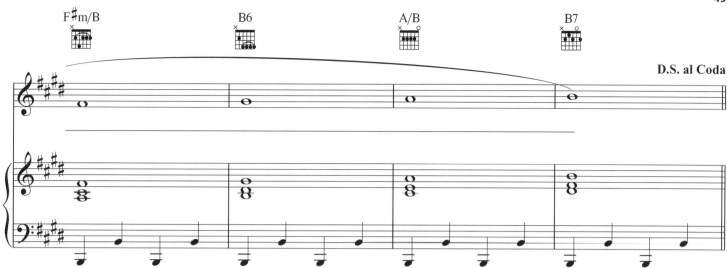

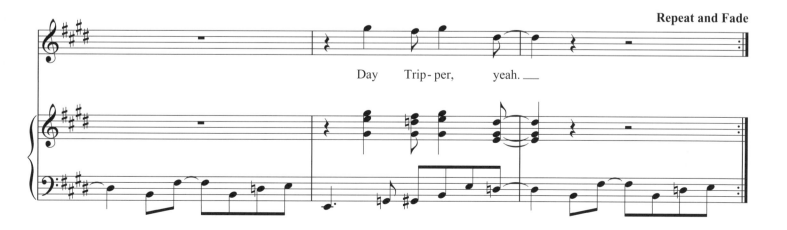

EIGHT DAYS A WEEK

Words and Music by JOHN LENNON
and PAUL McCARTNEY

Brightly, with a Swing feel

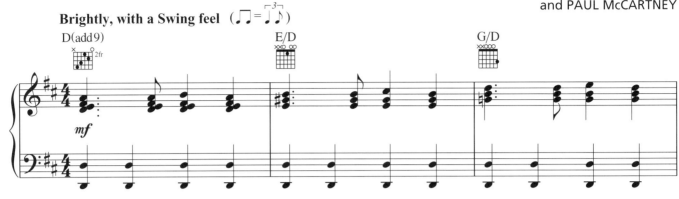

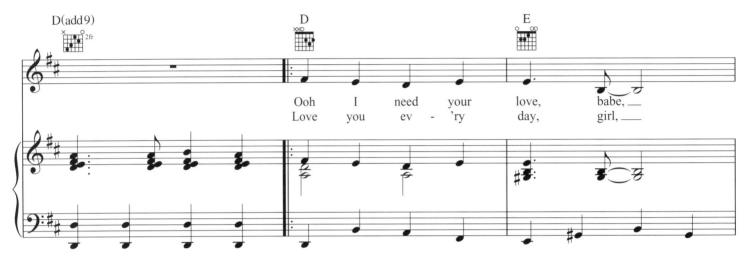

Ooh I need your love, babe,
Love you ev - 'ry day, girl,

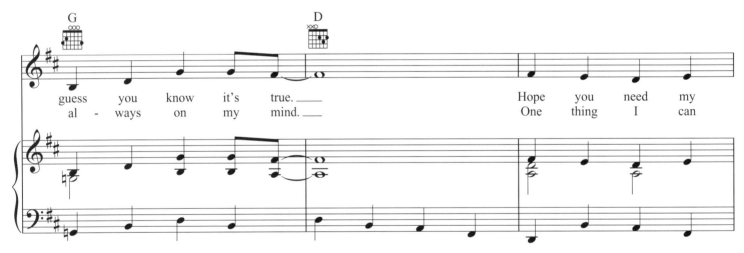

guess you know it's true. Hope you need my
al - ways on my mind. One thing I can

love, babe, just like I need you.
say, girl, love you all the time.

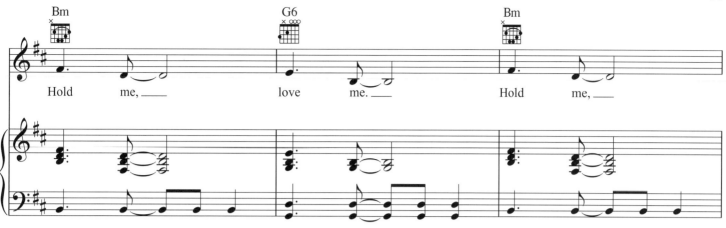

Hold me, ___ love me. ___ Hold me, ___

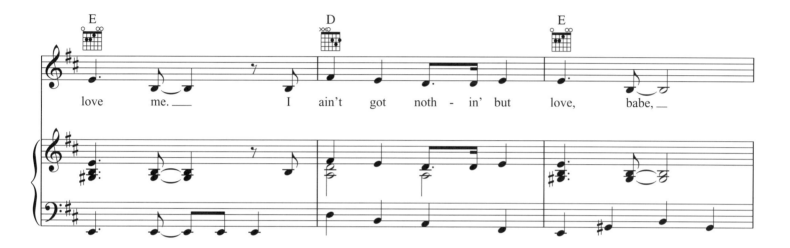

love me. ___ I ain't got noth-in' but love, babe, ___

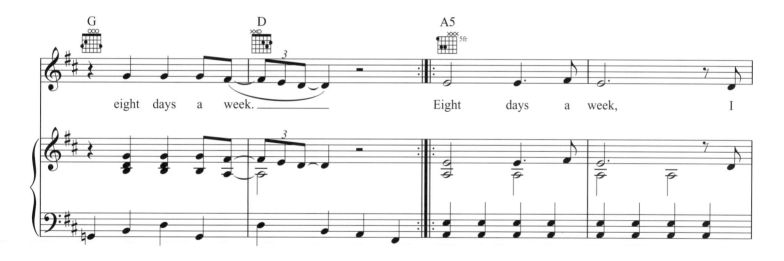

eight days a week. _____ Eight days a week, I

love _____ you. ___ Eight days a week is

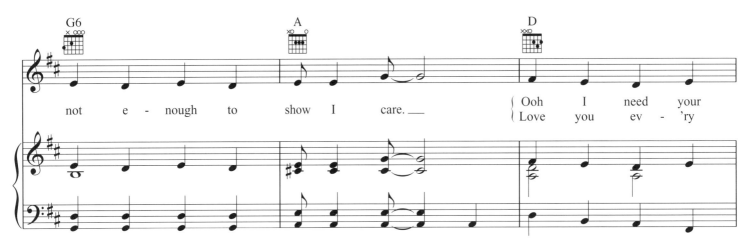

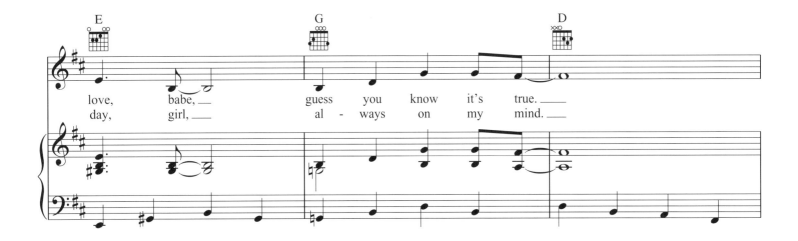

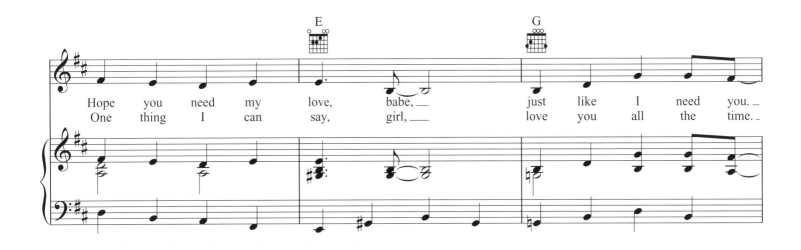

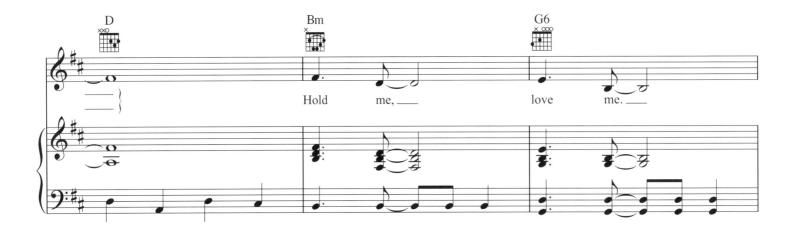

Hold me, ___ love me. ___ I ain't got noth - in' but

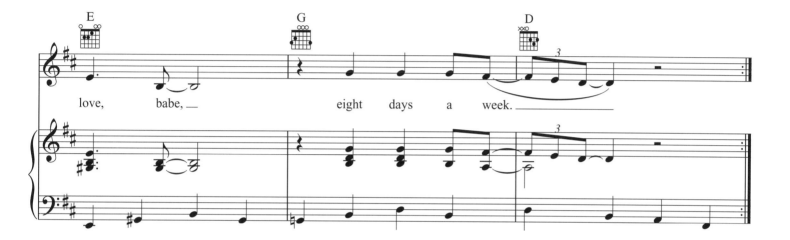

love, babe, ___ eight days a week. ___

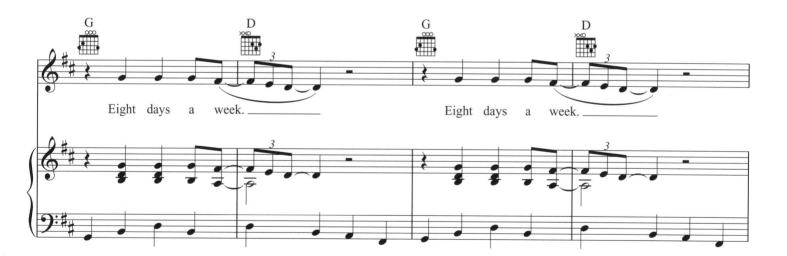

Eight days a week. ___ Eight days a week. ___

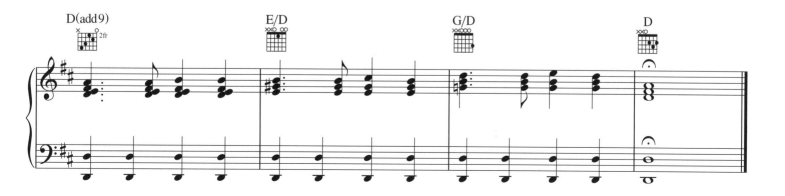

THE END

Words and Music by JOHN LENNON
and PAUL McCARTNEY

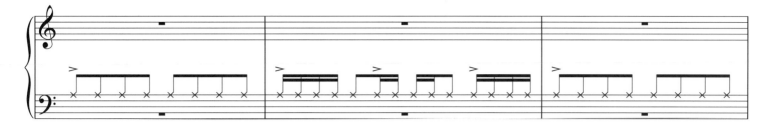

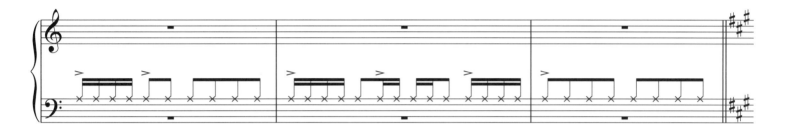

Love you, ___ love you, ___

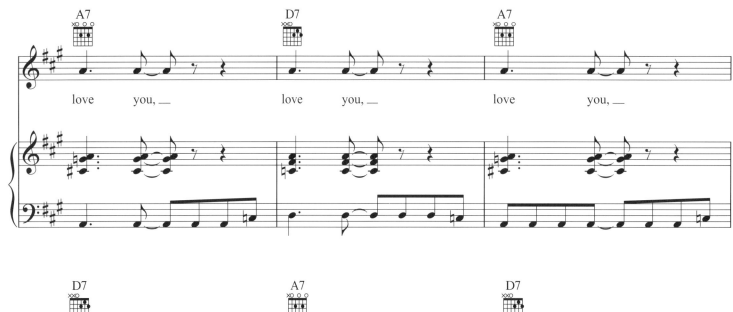

love you, ___ love you, ___ love you, ___

love you, ___ love you, ___ love you, ___

love you, ___ love you, ___ love you, ___

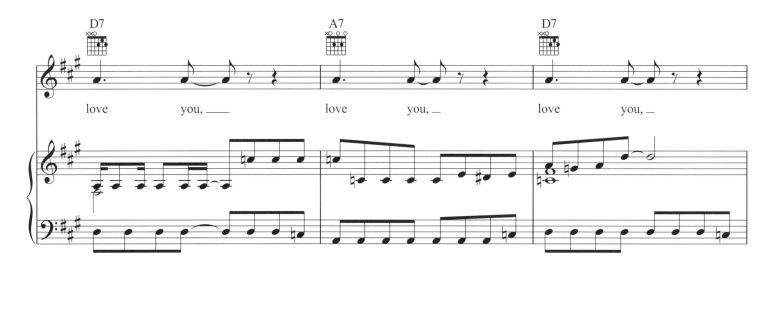

love you, ___ love you, ___ love you, ___

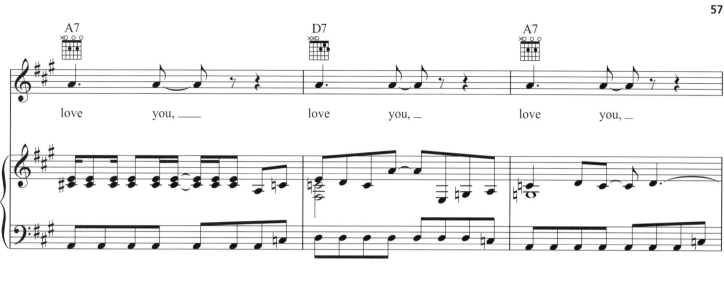

love you, ___ love you, __ love you, __

love you, __ love you, ___ love you, __

love you, __ love you, __ love you, __

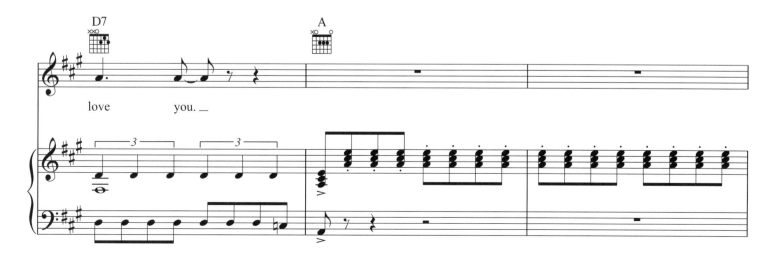

love you. __

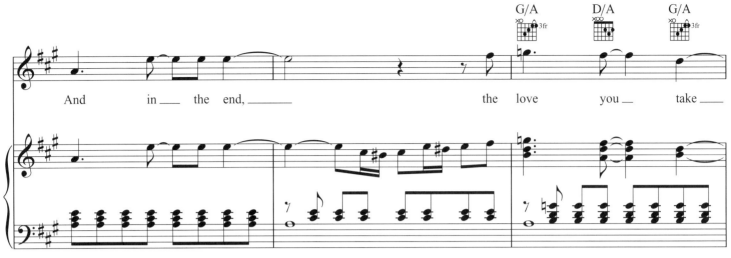

And in ___ the end, _____ the love you ___ take ___

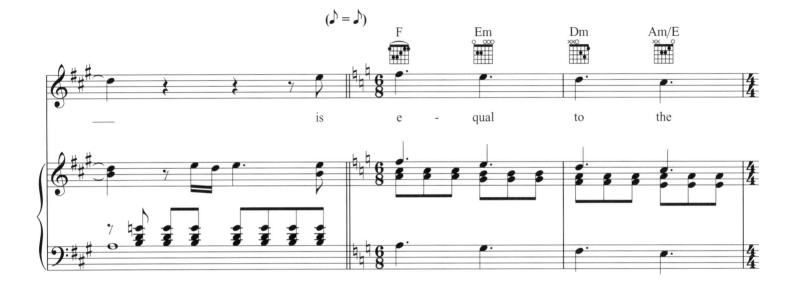

___ is e - qual to the

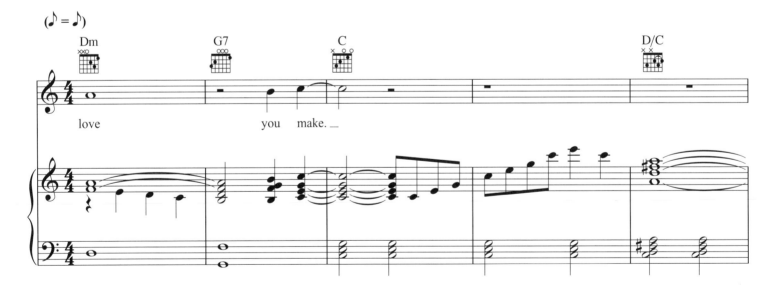

love you make. ___

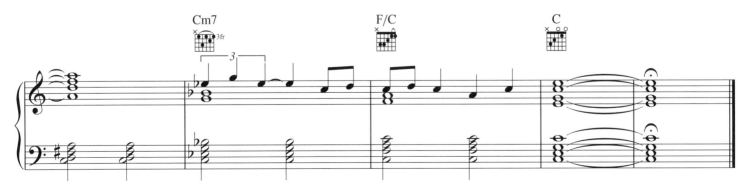

GET BACK

Words and Music by JOHN LENNON
and PAUL McCARTNEY

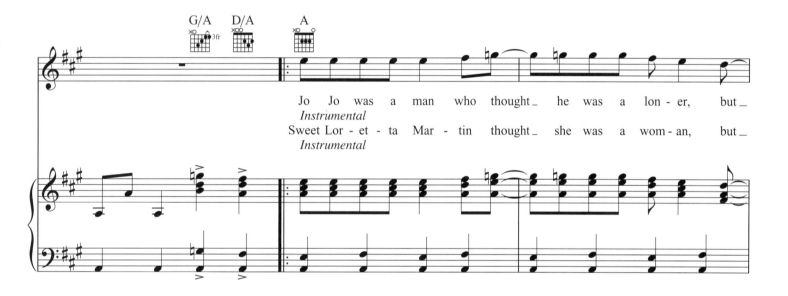

Jo Jo was a man who thought _ he was a lon - er, but _
Instrumental
Sweet Lor - et - ta Mar - tin thought _ she was a wom - an, but _
Instrumental

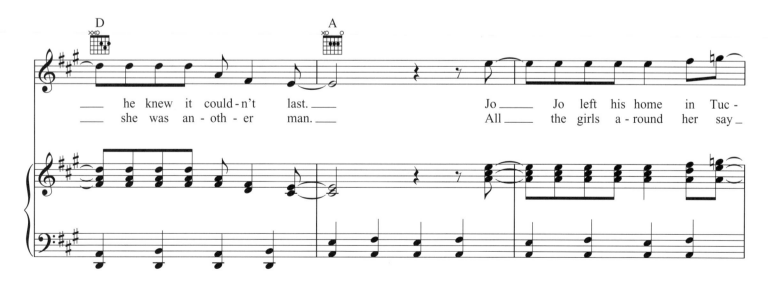

_ he knew it could - n't last. _
_ she was an - oth - er man. _
Jo _ Jo left his home in Tuc -
All _ the girls a - round her say _

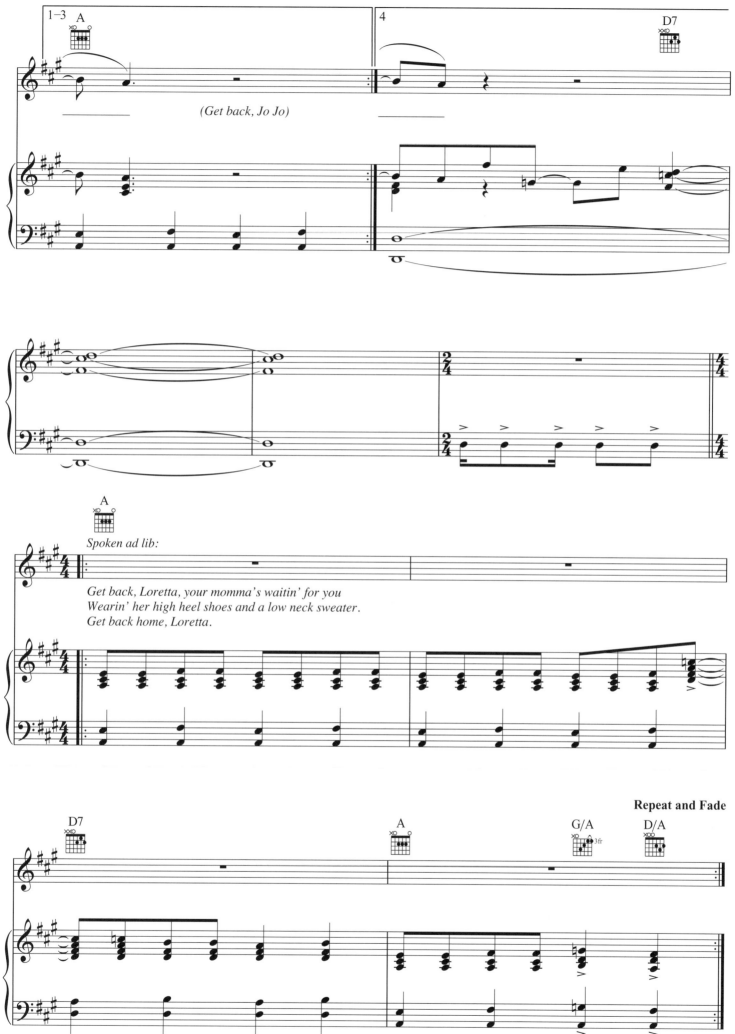

(Get back, Jo Jo)

Spoken ad lib:

Get back, Loretta, your momma's waitin' for you
Wearin' her high heel shoes and a low neck sweater.
Get back home, Loretta.

Repeat and Fade

GOLDEN SLUMBERS

Words and Music by JOHN LENNON
and PAUL McCARTNEY

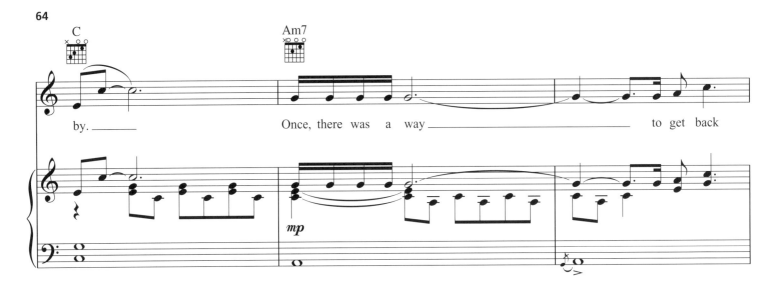

by. _____ Once, there was a way _____ to get back

home - ward. _____ Once, there was a way _____ to get back home. _____ Sleep, pret - ty dar - ling, do not cry, and I will sing a lull - a - by. _____

HELTER SKELTER

Words and Music by JOHN LENNON
and PAUL McCARTNEY

Moderate Rock

When I get to the bot-tom I go back to the top of the slide, __ where I stop and I turn and I go for a ride, __ till I get to the bot-tom, and I see you a-gain. __

Yeah, yeah, yeah, _____ yeah! But do you, don't you want _____ me to love _____ you? I'm com - ing down fast, but I'm miles a - bove _____ you. Tell me, tell me, tell _____ me, come on, tell _____ me the an - swer. _____

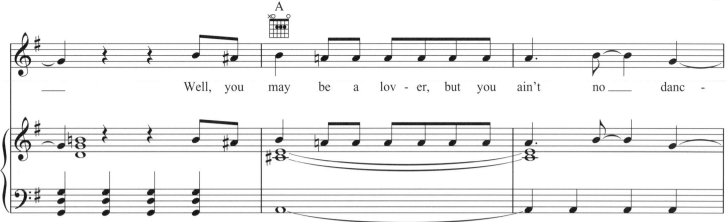

Well, you may be a lov-er, but you ain't no ___ danc -

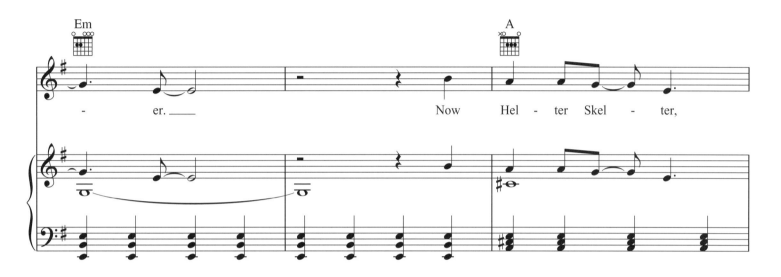

- er. ___ Now Hel - ter Skel - ter,

Hel - ter Skel - ter,

Hel - ter Skel - ter, ye - ah! ___

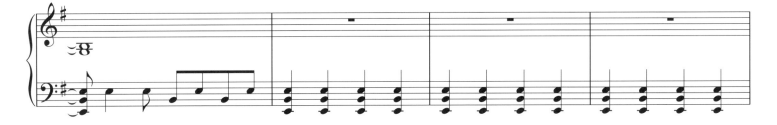

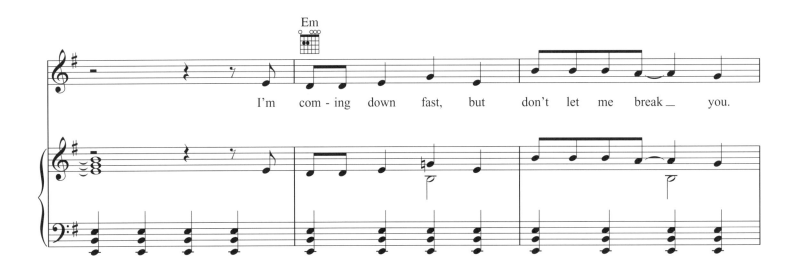

Well, will you, won't you want __ me to make __ you?
do you, don't you want __ me to make __ you?

I'm com- ing down fast, but don't let me break __ you.

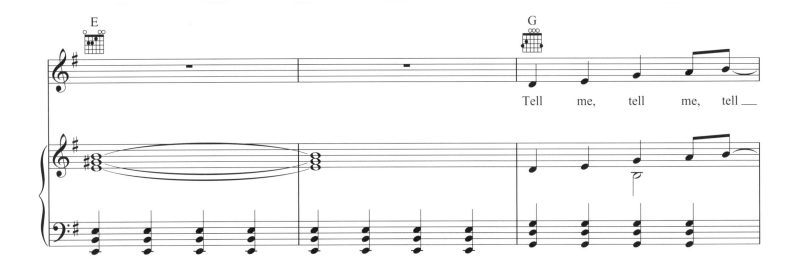

Tell me, tell me, tell __

me___ the an - swer. You may be a lov-er, but you ain't no danc - er.

Look out! ___ Hel - ter Skel - ter,

Hel - ter Skel - ter,

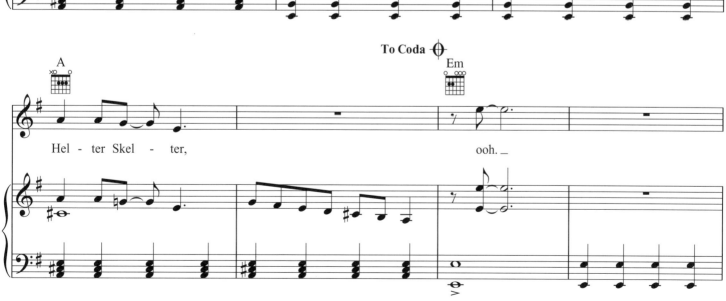

Hel - ter Skel - ter, ooh. ___

Look out! 'Cause here she comes!

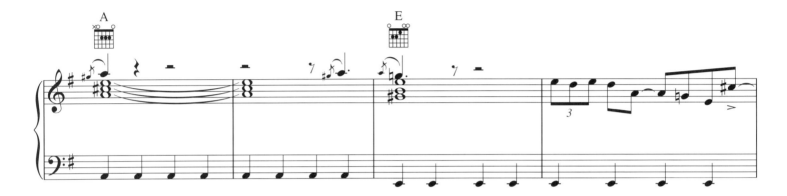

When I

get   to the bot-tom I go back   to the top of the slide, ___ and I stop and I

turn and I go for a ride, ___ and I get to the bot - tom, and I see you a - gain. ___

D.S. al Coda

Yeah, yeah, yeah, ___ yeah! Well,

CODA

(Shout, ad lib:) Look out! Helter Skelter!

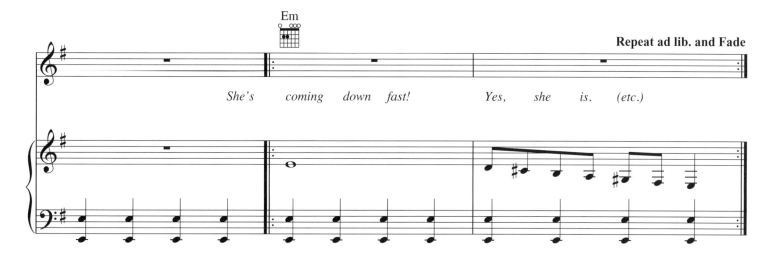

Repeat ad lib. and Fade

She's coming down fast! Yes, she is. (etc.)

HERE TODAY

Words and Music by
PAUL McCARTNEY

be - fore, and I am hold - ing back the

tears no more, _ ooh ooh

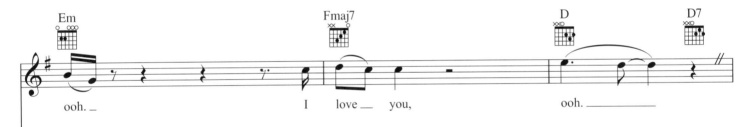

ooh. _ I love _ you, ooh. _____

What a - bout the time we met? _ Well, I sup - pose that you could say that we were play - ing hard _ to get.

HI, HI, HI

Words and Music by PAUL McCARTNEY
and LINDA McCARTNEY

Well: When I met you at the sta - tion __ you were

stand - ing with a boot - leg in your hand __ We went to

my lit - tle place __ for a taste __ of __ a mul - ti-col-oured band. __

We're gon - na get hi, hi, _____ hi, _____ the night is _____ young. _

_____ She'll be my funk - y lit-tle ma - ma gon-na rock _

_____ it and we've on - ly just be - gun. _____ We're gon - na get

hi, hi, _____ hi _____ with the mu - sic _____ on. _____

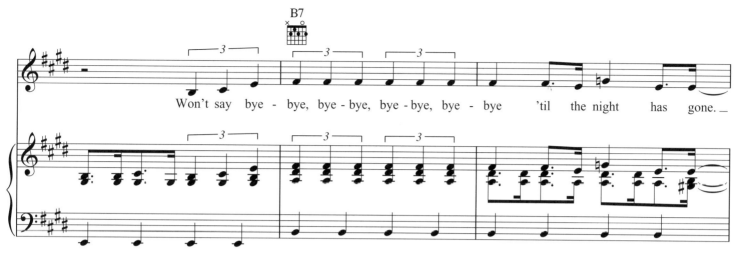

Won't say bye - bye, bye - bye, bye - bye, bye - bye 'til the night has gone.

I'm gon - na do it to you, gon - na do you, sweet ba-

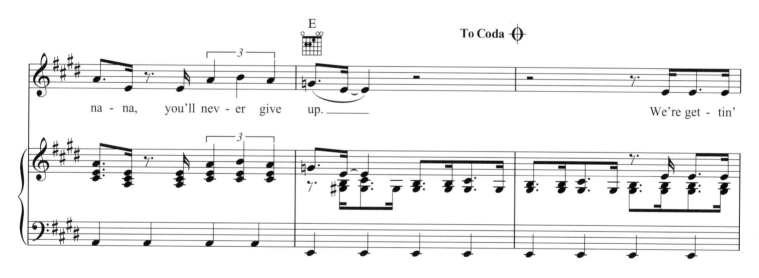

na - na, you'll nev - er give up. We're get - tin'

hi, hi, hi in the mid - day sun.

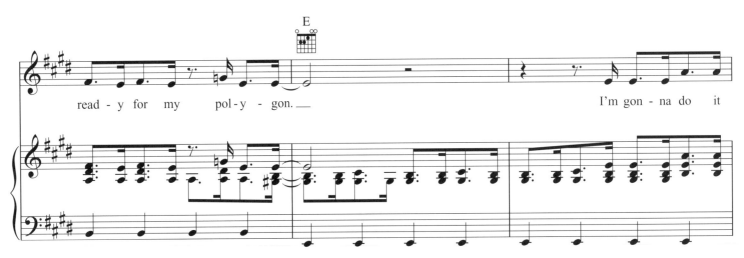

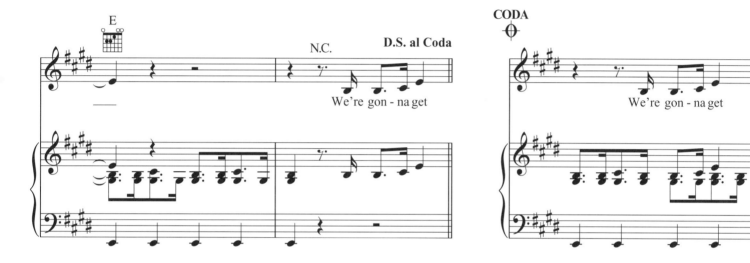

HEY JUDE

Words and Music by JOHN LENNON
and PAUL McCARTNEY

Hey Jude,_____ don't make it bad; take a
don't make it bad; take a

sad song_____ and make it bet - ter._____ Re -
sad song_____ and make it bet - ter._____ Re -

mem - ber to let her in - to your heart; then you can start_____
mem - ber to let her un - der your skin, then you be - gin_____

To Coda

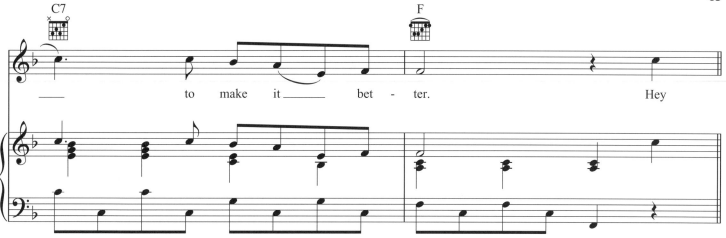

to make it _____ bet - ter.   Hey

Jude, _____ don't be a - fraid.   You were made to _____ go out and
Jude, _____ don't let me down.   You have found her, _____ now go and

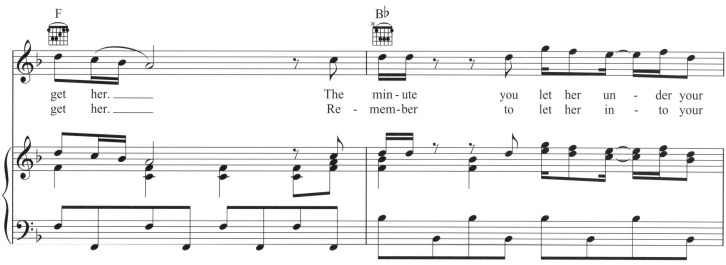

get her. _____   The min - ute   you let her un - der your
get her. _____   Re - mem - ber   to let her in - to your

skin,   then you be - gin _____   to make it _____ bet - ter.
heart;   then you can start _____   to make it _____ bet - ter.

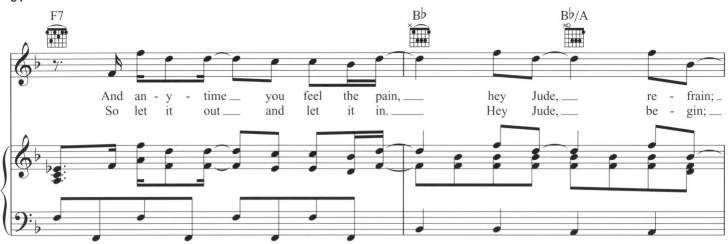

And an-y-time ___ you feel the pain, ___ hey Jude, ___ re - frain; ___
So let it out ___ and let it in. ___ Hey Jude, ___ be - gin; ___

___ don't car - ry the world ___ up - on ___ your shoul - ders. ___
___ you're wait - ing for some - one to ___ per - form ___ with. ___

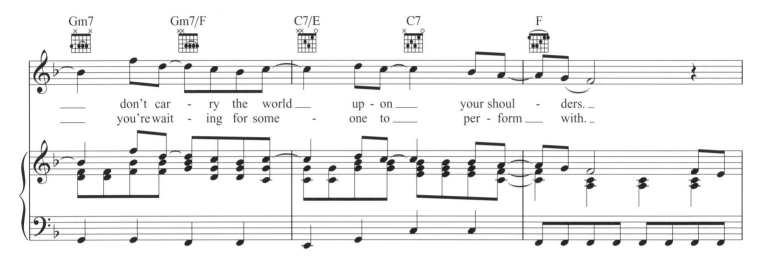

For well you know ___ that it's a fool ___ who plays ___ it cool ___
And don't you know ___ that it's just you? ___ Hey Jude, ___ you'll do. ___

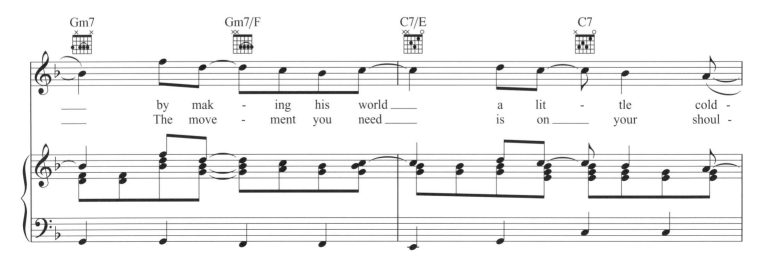

___ by mak - ing his world ___ a lit - tle cold -
___ The move - ment you need ___ is on ___ your shoul -

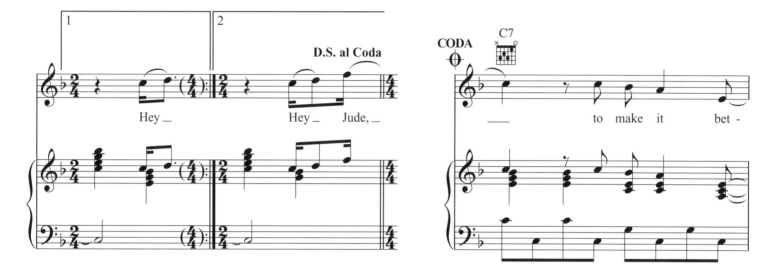

I SAW HER STANDING THERE

Words and Music by JOHN LENNON
and PAUL McCARTNEY

how could I dance ____ with an - oth - er, woo, ____
She would-n't dance ____ with an - oth - er, woo, ____

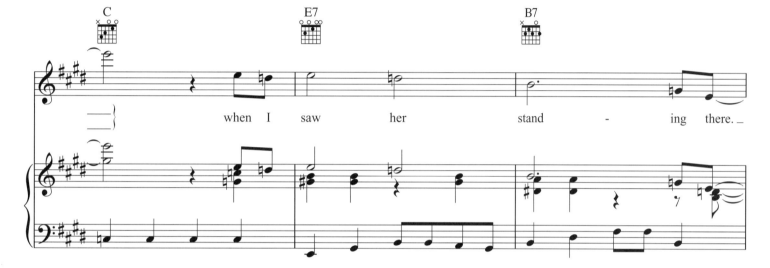

when I saw her stand - ing there. ____

Well, she ____ Well, my

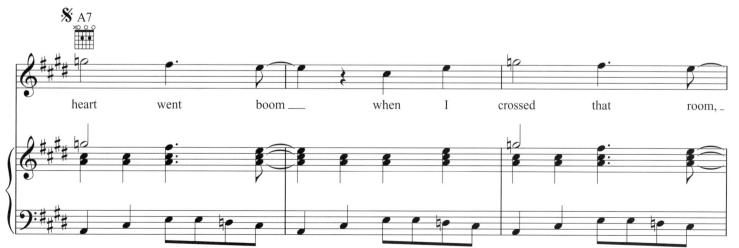

heart went boom ____ when I crossed that room, ____

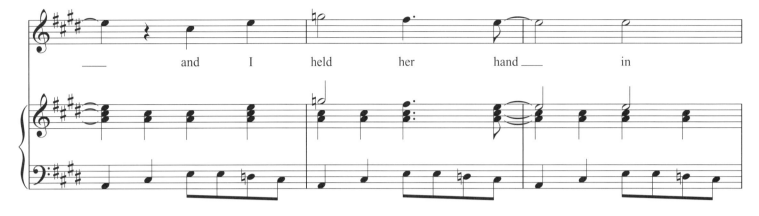

and I held her hand ___ in

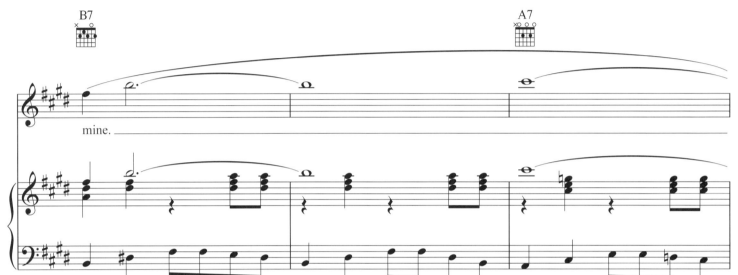

B7   A7

mine. _____

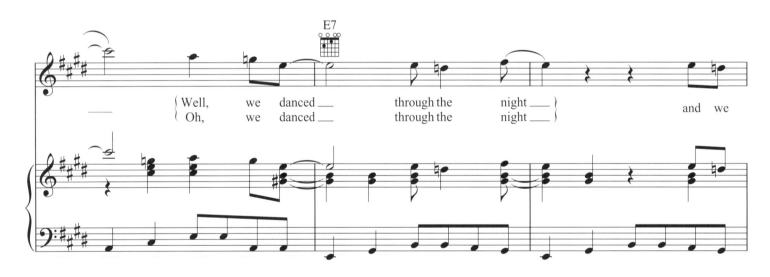

E7

{ Well, we danced ___ through the night ___ }
{ Oh, we danced ___ through the night ___ }

and we

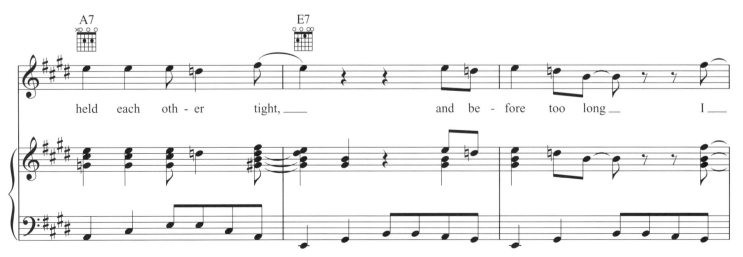

A7   E7

held each oth-er tight, ___   and be-fore too long ___ I ___

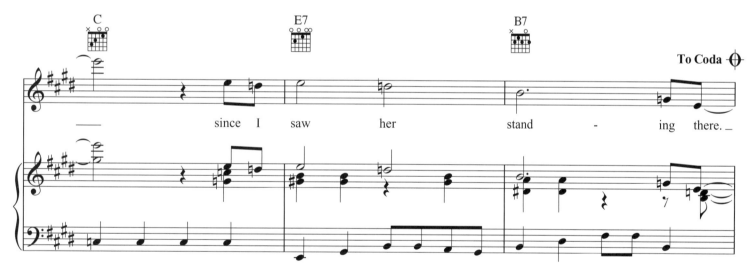

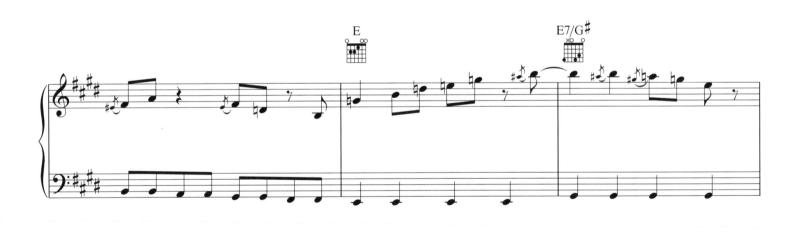

D.S. al Coda

Well, my

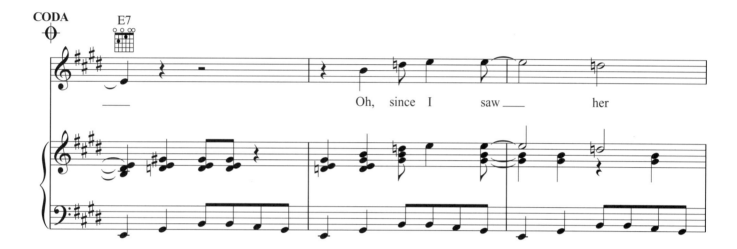

CODA

Oh, since I saw __ her

stand - ing there. __ Yeah, well, since I saw __ her

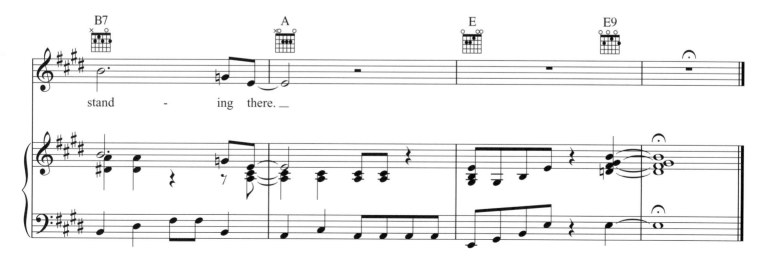

stand - ing there. __

I'VE JUST SEEN A FACE

Words and Music by JOHN LENNON
and PAUL McCARTNEY

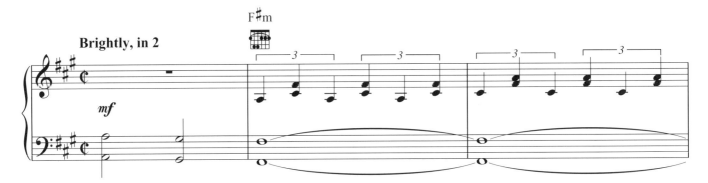

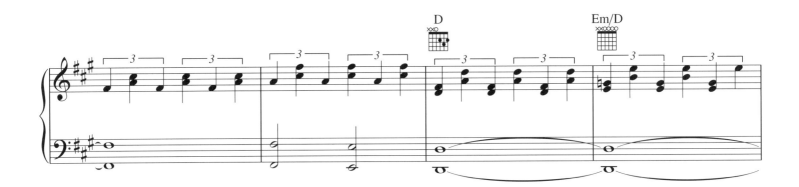

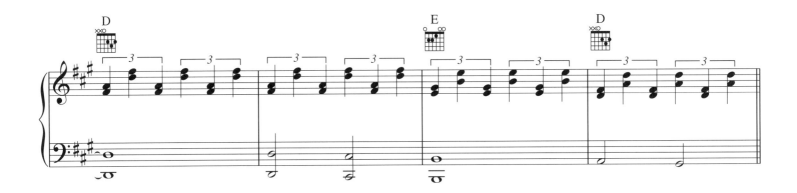

I've just seen a face, I can't for-get the time ___ or

place where we just met. She's just the girl _____ for me and I _____

_____ want all the world to see _____ we've met. Mm mm

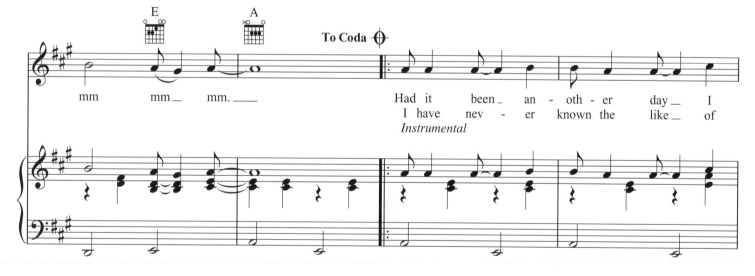

mm mm ____ mm. ____

To Coda ⊕

Had it been an-oth-er day ____ I
I have nev - er known the like ____ of
Instrumental

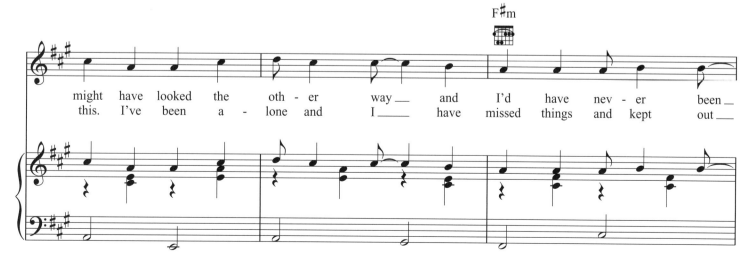

might have looked the oth-er way ____ and I'd have nev-er been ____
this. I've been a - lone and I ____ have missed things and kept out ____

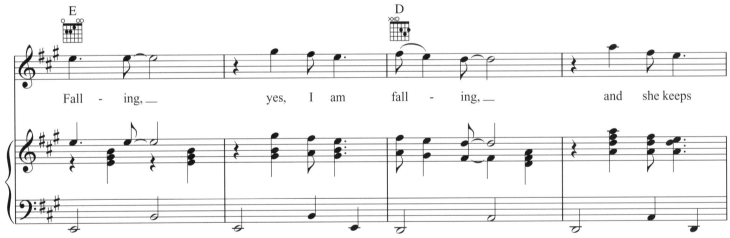

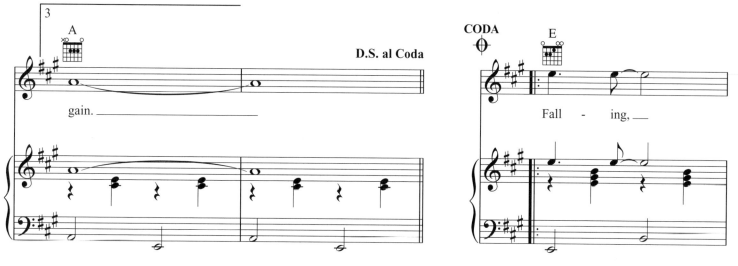

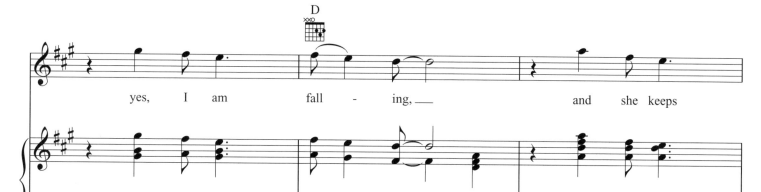

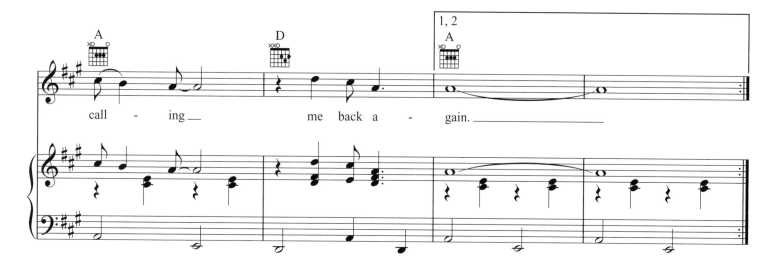

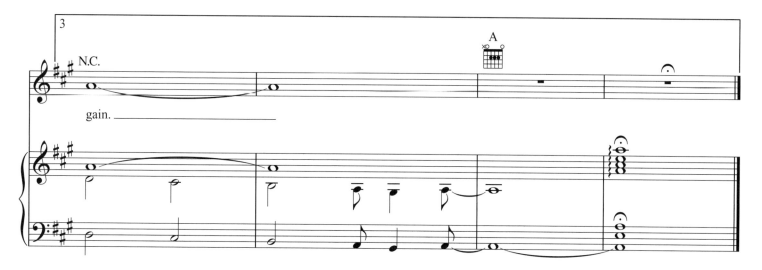

JUNIOR'S FARM

Words and Music by PAUL McCARTNEY
and LINDA McCARTNEY

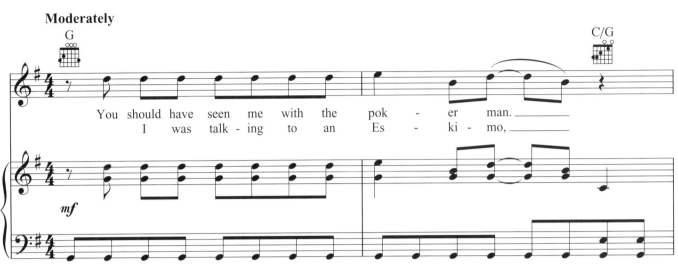

You should have seen me with the pok - er man. ___
I was talk - ing to an Es - ki - mo, ___

I had a hon - ey and I bet a grand, ___ just ___ in the nick of time I
said he was hop - ing for a fall of snow, ___ when up popped a sea lion

looked at his hand. ___
read - y to go. ___

Let's

go, let's go, let's go, let's go ___ down ___ to Ju-nior's Farm where I

want to lay low. ___ Low ___ life, high life; oh, let's go, ___ take ___

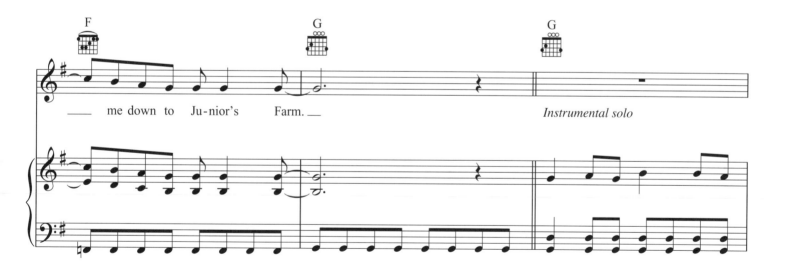

___ me down to Ju-nior's Farm. ___

Instrumental solo

At the Hous-es of
I took my bag in-to a

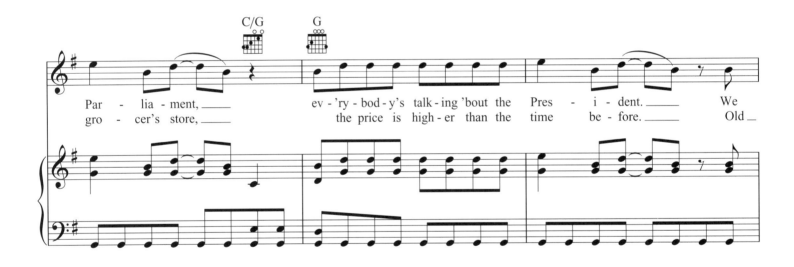

Par - lia - ment,_____ ev-'ry-bod-y's talk-ing 'bout the Pres - i - dent._____ We
gro - cer's store,_____ the price is high-er than the time be - fore._____ Old_

all chip in for a bag of ce - ment._____
___ man asked me why is it more?_____

I

Ol - ly Har - dy should have had more sense, _____ he bought a gee - gee and he
said you should have seen me with the pok - er man. _____ I had a hon - ey and I

jumped the fence, _____ all _____ for the sake of a cou - ple of pence. _____
bet a grand, _____ just _____ in the nick of time I looked at his hand. _____

Let's go, let's go, let's go, let's go _____ down _____ to Ju - nior's Farm where I

want to lay low. _ Low _____ life, high life; oh, let's go, _____ take _____

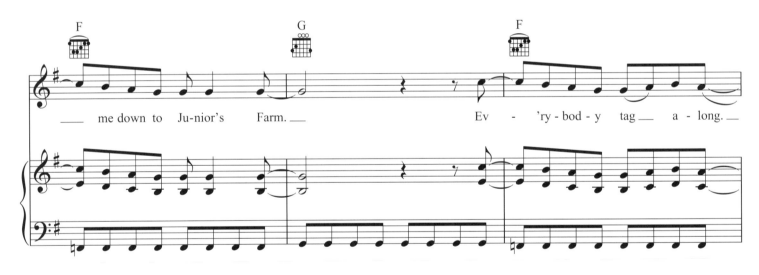

LET IT BE

Words and Music by JOHN LENNON
and PAUL McCARTNEY

When I find my-self ___ in times of trou-ble,
Instrumental

Moth-er Mar - y comes to me speak-ing words of wis-dom; let it

be. ___ And in my hour of dark - ness, she is

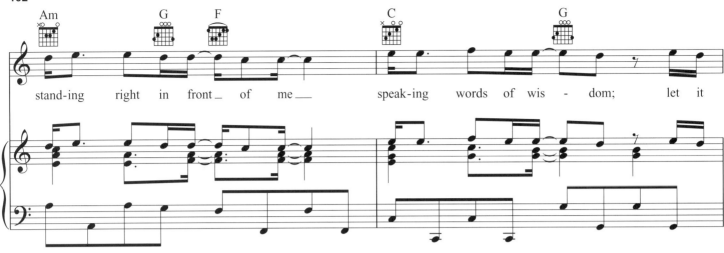

stand-ing right in front of me speak-ing words of wis - dom; let it

be. *Instrumental ends* Let it be, let it be, let it be,

let it be. Whis-per words of wis - dom; let it be.

And when the bro - ken - heart - ed peo - ple
And when the night is cloud - y, there is

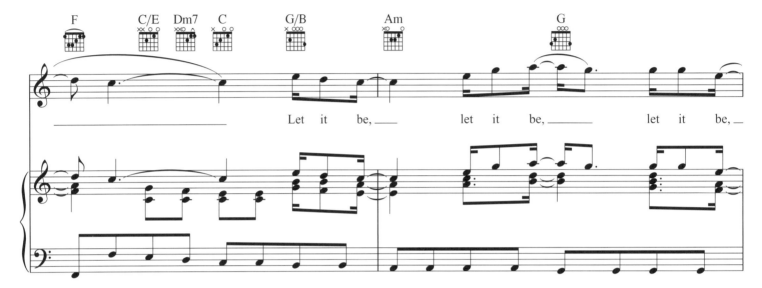

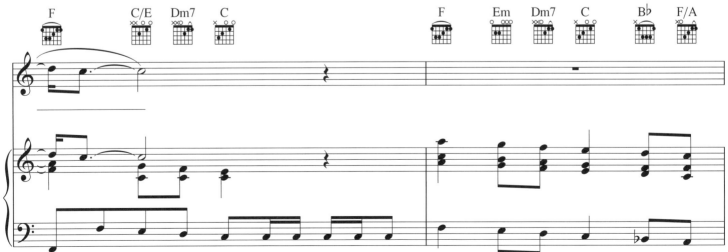

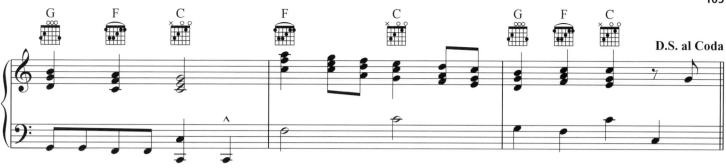

D.S. al Coda

CODA

Let it be, ___ let it be, _____ let it be, _

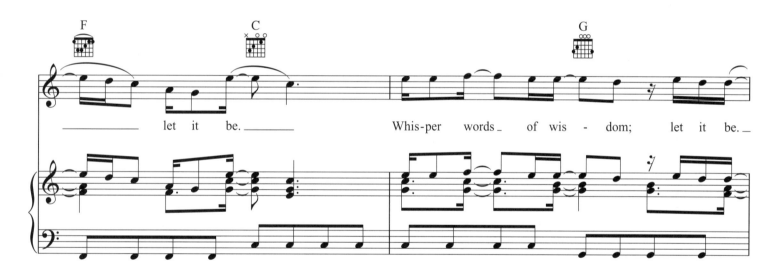

_____ let it be. _____ Whis-per words_ of wis - dom; let it be. _

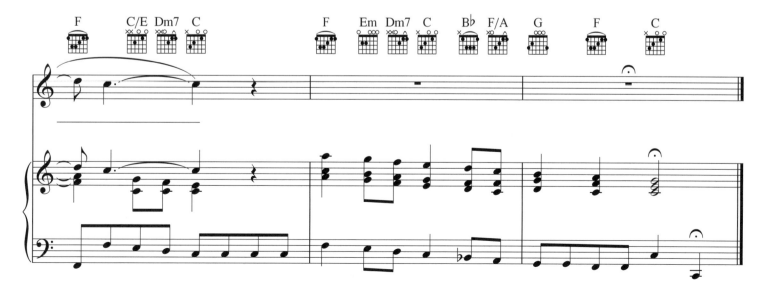

LADY MADONNA

Words and Music by JOHN LENNON
and PAUL McCARTNEY

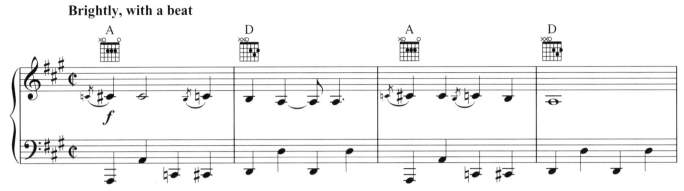

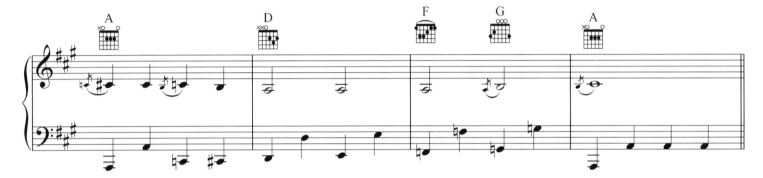

La - dy Ma - don - na, chil - dren at your feet,
La - dy Ma - don - na, ba - by at your breast,
La - dy Ma - don - na, ly - ing on the bed,
La - dy Ma - don - na, chil - dren at your feet,

Won - der how you man - age to make
Won - ders how you man - age to feed
Lis - ten to the mu - sic play - ing
Won - der how you man - age to make

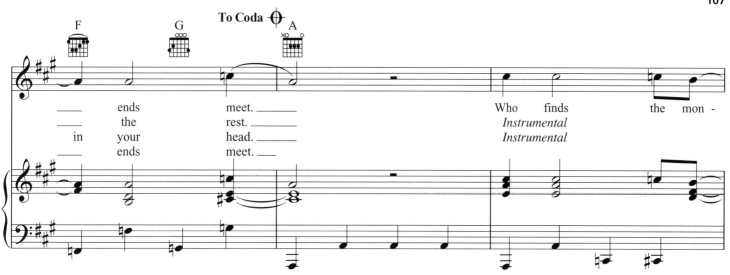

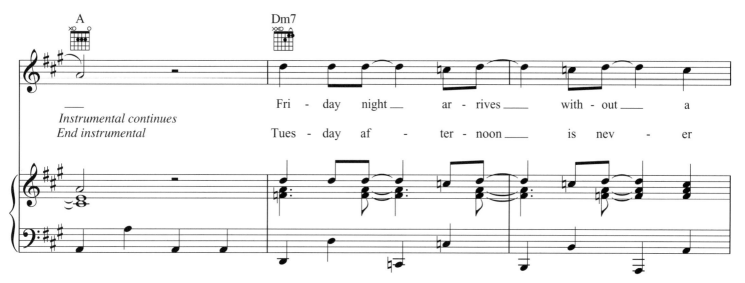

suit - case, _____ Sun - day morn - ing,
end - ing, _____ Wednes - day morn - ing,

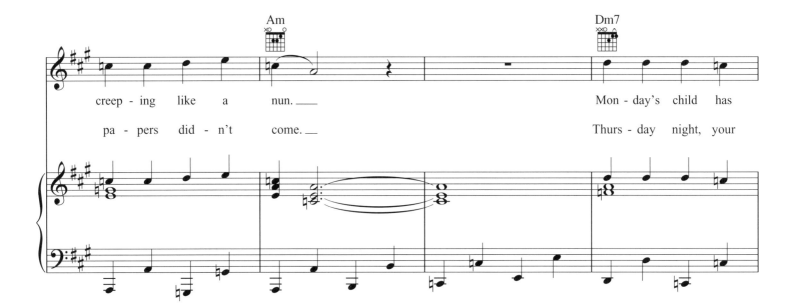

creep - ing like a nun. _____ Mon - day's child has
pa - pers did - n't come. _____ Thurs - day night, your

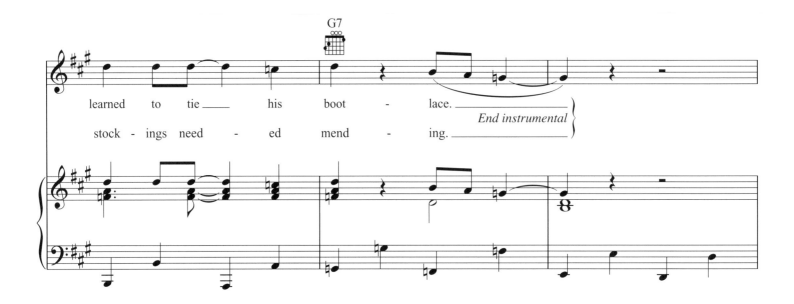

learned to tie _____ his boot - lace. _____
stock - ings need - ed mend - ing. _____

End instrumental

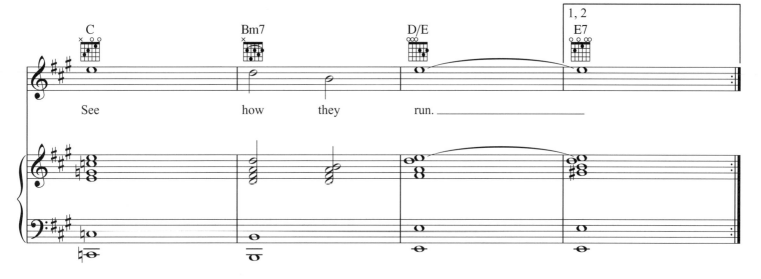

See how they run. _____

D.S. al Coda

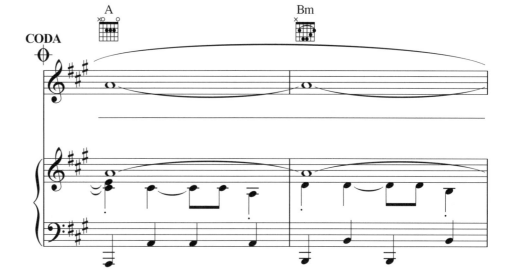

CODA

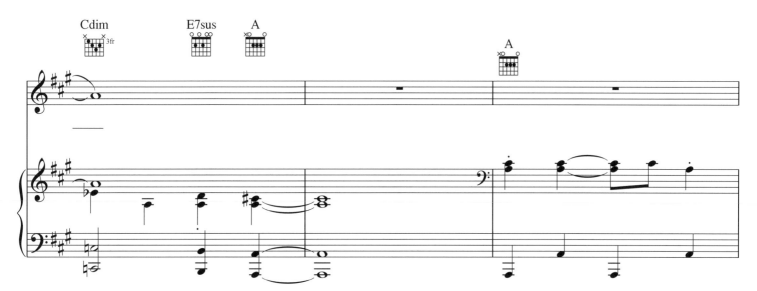

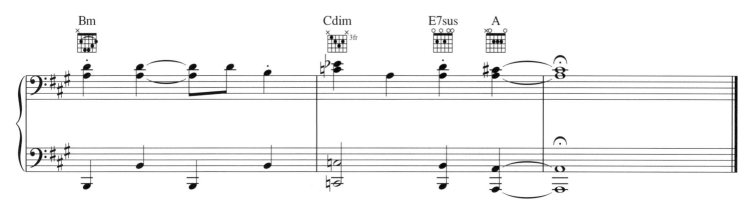

LET ME ROLL IT

Words and Music by
PAUL and LINDA McCARTNEY

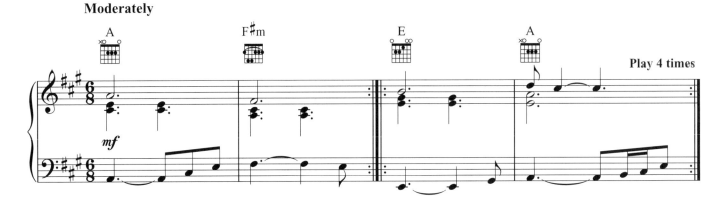

You gave me some - thing.   I un - der - stand,   you gave me
I wan - na tell you,   and now's the time.   I wan - na

lov - ing in the palm of my hand.
tell you that you're go - ing to me mine.

I can't tell you how I feel. My

heart is like __ a wheel. Let me roll it, ___ let me roll it to you. __ Let me

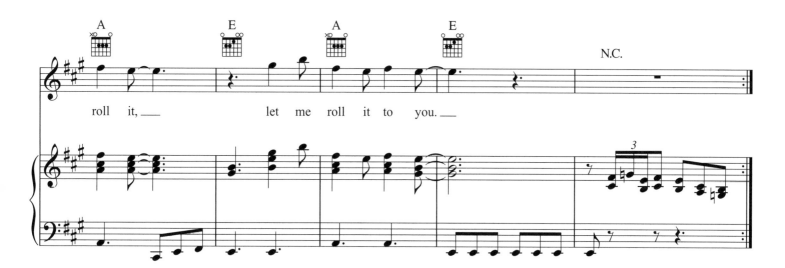

roll it, ___ let me roll it to you. __

Repeat and Fade   **Optional Ending**

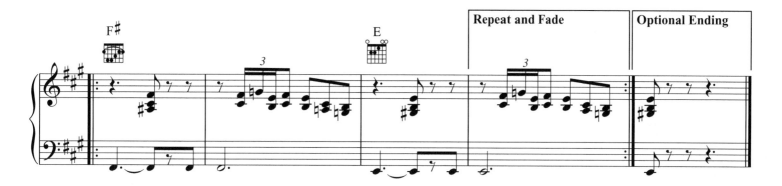

LISTEN TO WHAT THE MAN SAID

Words and Music by PAUL McCARTNEY
and LINDA McCARTNEY

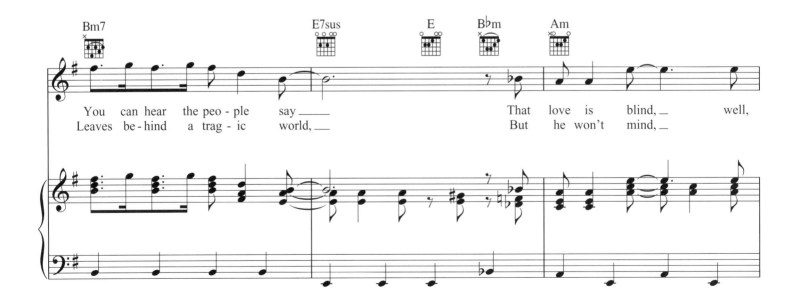

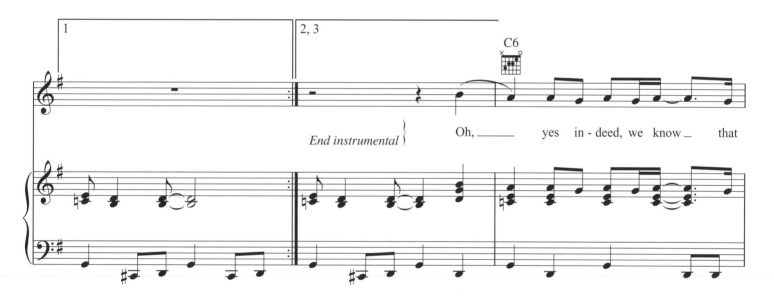

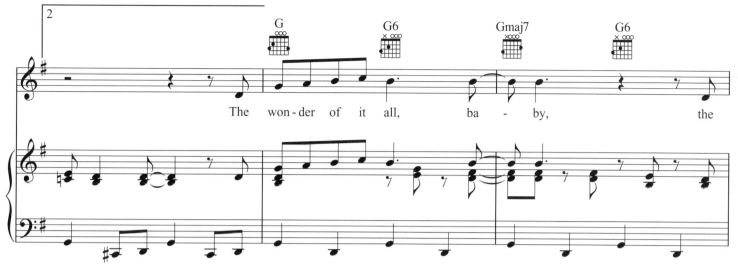

The won-der of it all, ba - by, the

won-der of it all, ba - by, the won-der of it all, ba -

- by, yeah, yeah, yeah.

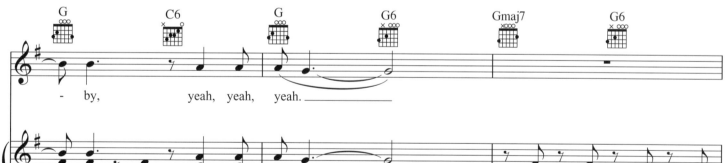

rall.

LIVE AND LET DIE

Words and Music by PAUL McCARTNEY
and LINDA McCARTNEY

When you were young and your heart was an o-pen book, _
Instrumental
End instrumental

you used to say live and let live.)
You used to say live and let live.)
(You know you did, you know you did, you know you

did.) __ But if this ev-er-chang-ing world in which we live in makes you

give in and cry, _____ say live and let die! _____

Live and let die, _____ live and let

die, _____ live and let die. _____

To Coda ⊕

What does it mat - ter to ya, when you got a job to do. __ You got - ta

do it well. __ You got - ta give the oth - er fel - low hell! _____

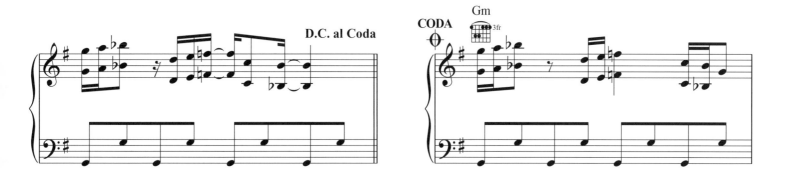

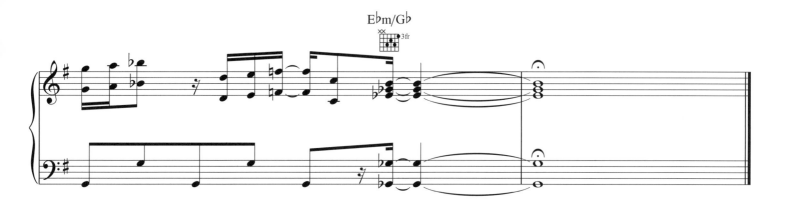

THE LONG AND WINDING ROAD

Words and Music by JOHN LENNON
and PAUL McCARTNEY

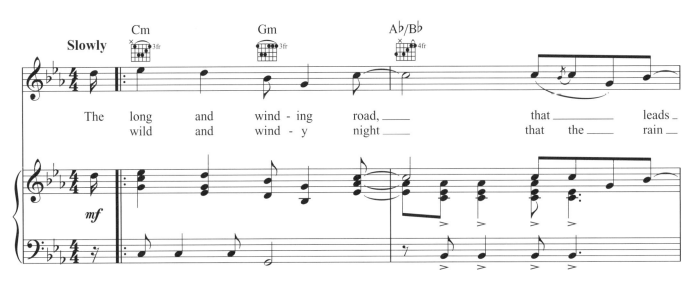

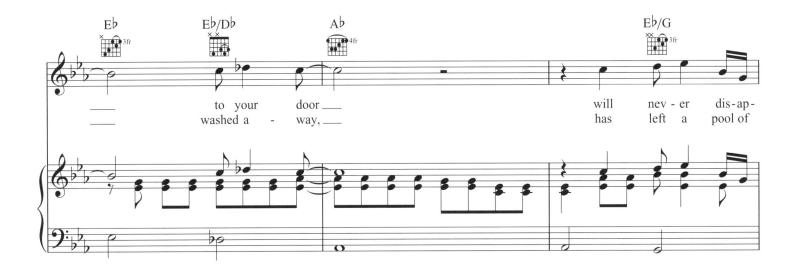

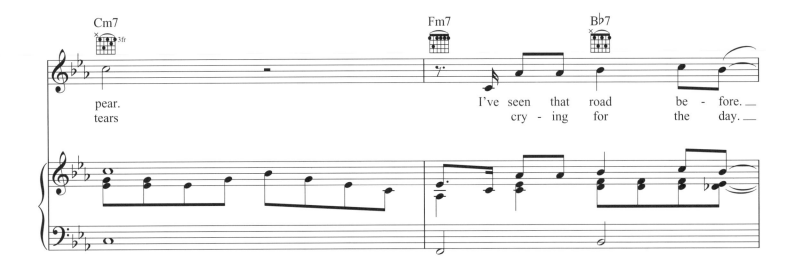

It al - ways leads ____
Why leave me stand - ing

____ me here. Lead me to your ____ door. The
here? Let me know the ____

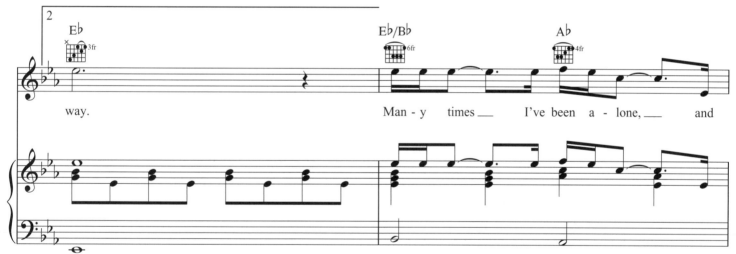

way. Man - y times ____ I've been a - lone, ____ and

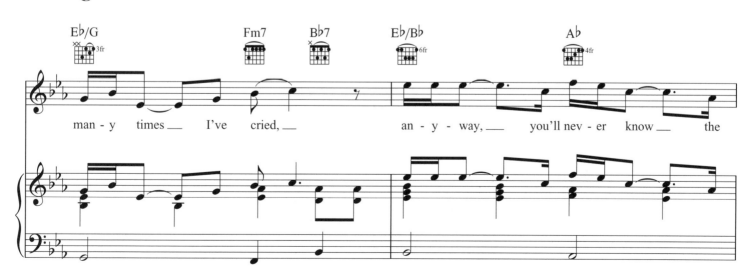

man - y times ____ I've cried, ____ an - y - way, ____ you'll nev - er know ____ the

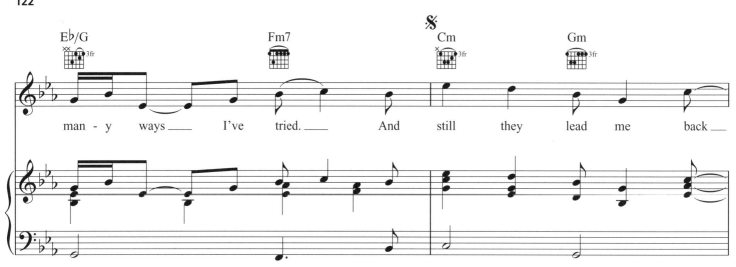

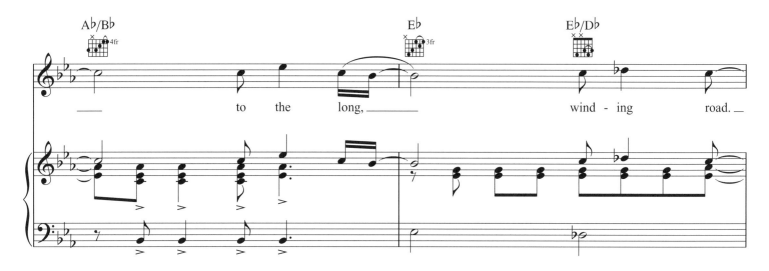

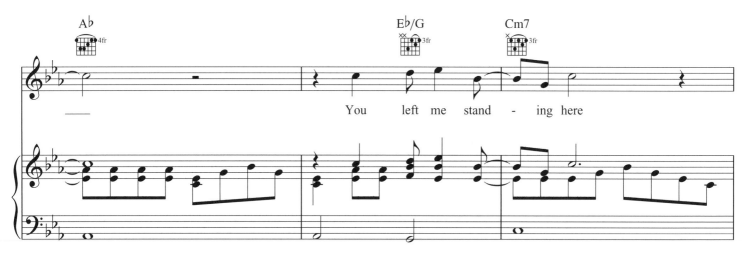

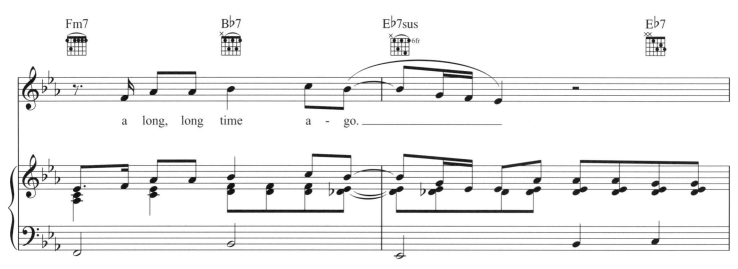

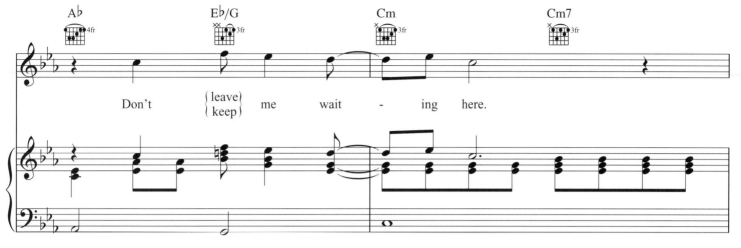

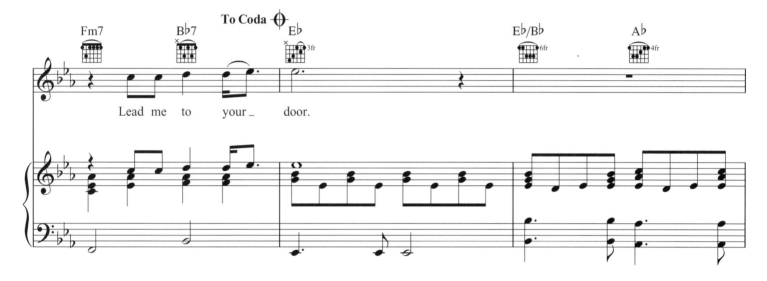

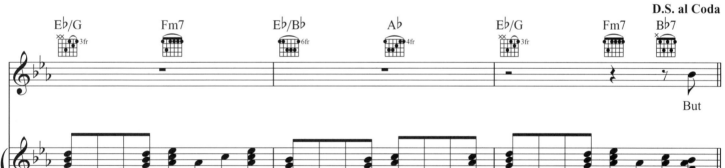

LOVELY RITA

Words and Music by JOHN LENNON
and PAUL McCARTNEY

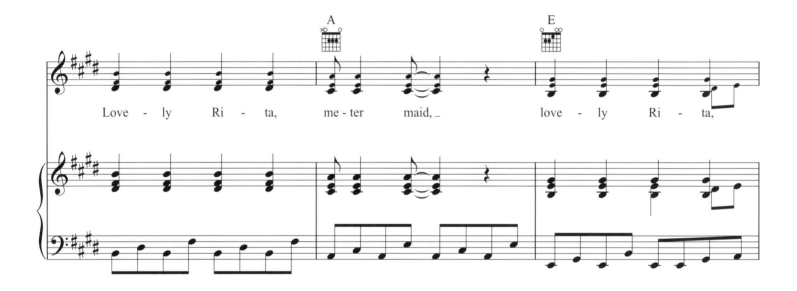

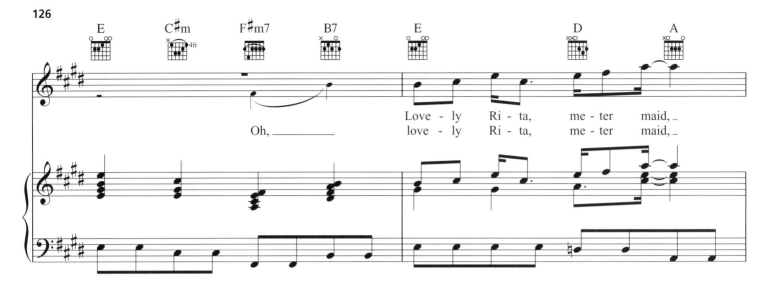

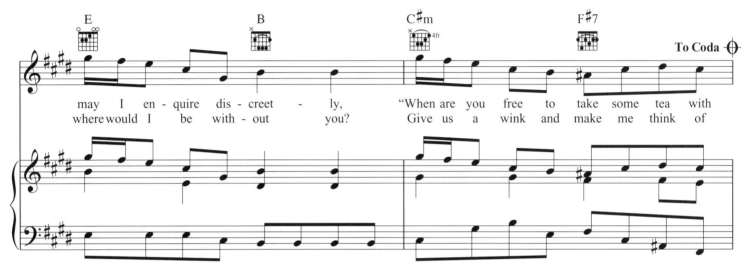

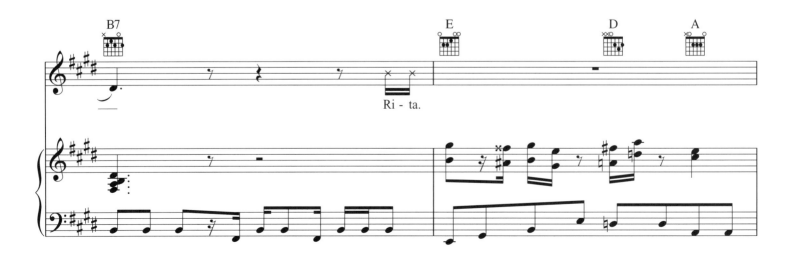

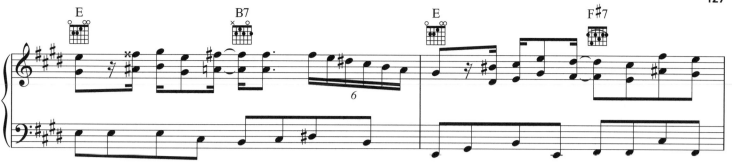

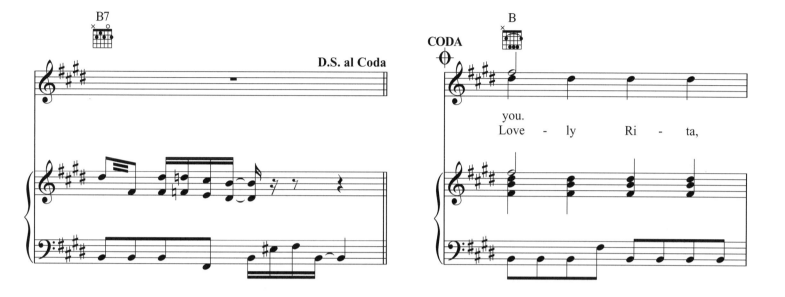

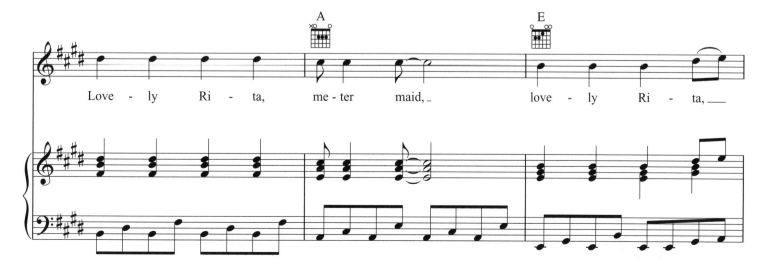

me - ter   maid. _

MAYBE I'M AMAZED

Words and Music by
PAUL McCARTNEY

(1.) Ba - by, I'm a - mazed at the way you love me all the time, _
(2.) Instrumental
(3.) May - be I'm a - mazed at the way you're with me all the time, _
(4.) Instrumental

and may - be I'm a - fraid of the way I love you.

and may - be I'm a - fraid of the way I need you.

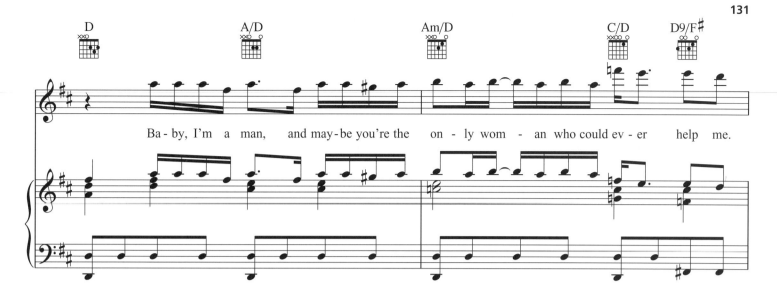

Ba-by, I'm a man, and may-be you're the on-ly wom-an who could ev-er help me.

Ba-by, won't you help me to un-der-stand? _ Ooh. _____

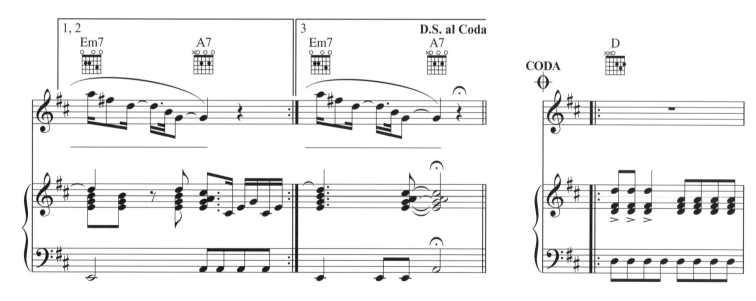

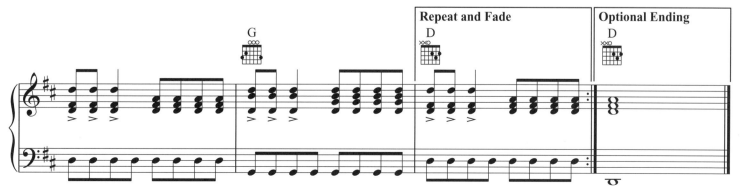

MRS. VANDEBILT

Words and Music by
PAUL and LINDA McCARTNEY

134

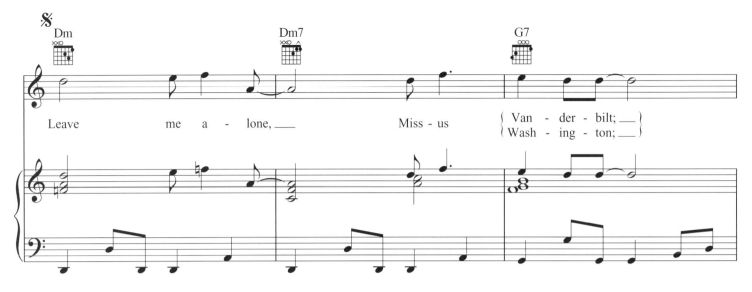

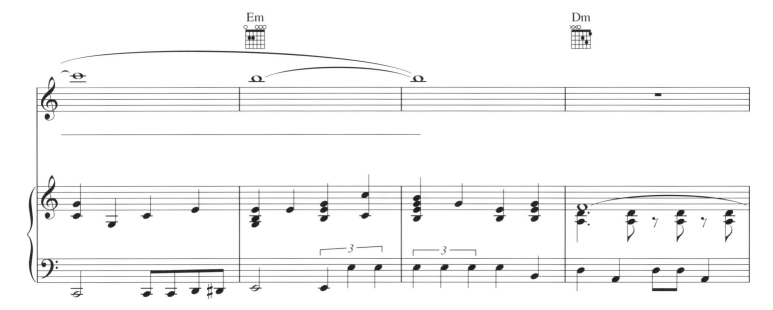

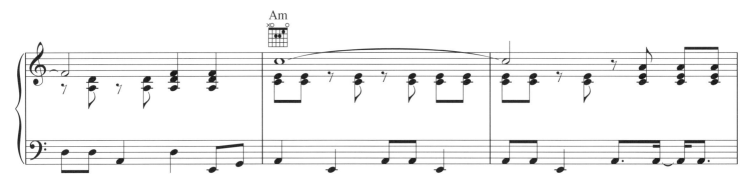

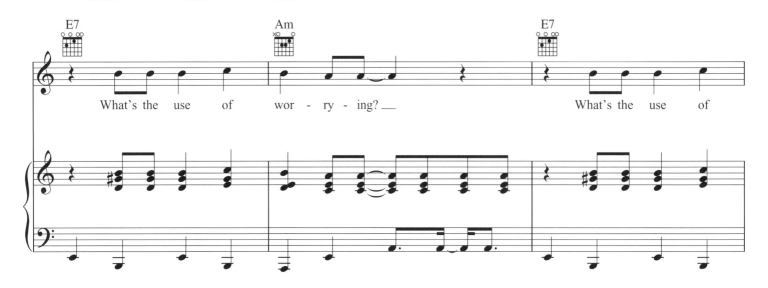

What's the use of wor - ry - ing? ___ What's the use of

MY VALENTINE

Words and Music by
PAUL McCARTNEY

Slowly

What if it rained? ___

(1.,3.) We did-n't care. ___
(2.) would pass me by, ___

She said that some-day soon, the sun was gon-na shine. ___
I'd tell my-self that I was wait-ing for a sign. ___

And she was right, ___ this love of mine, ___
Then she ap-peared, ___ a love so fine, ___

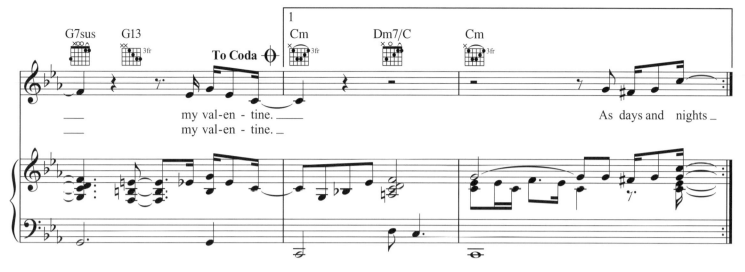

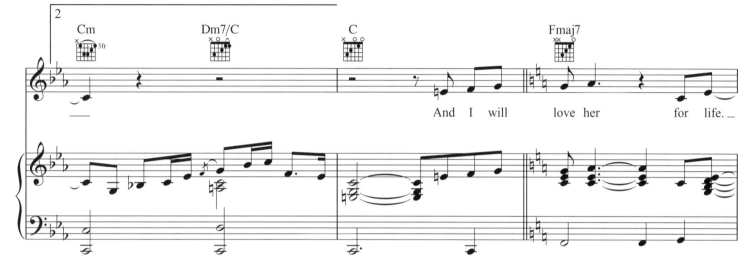

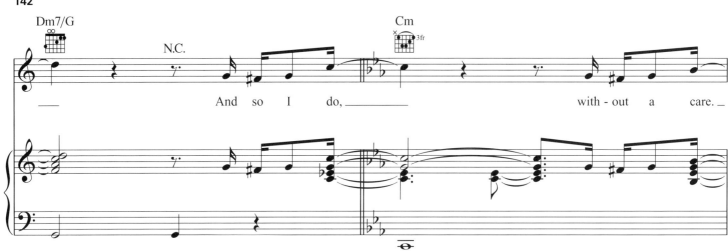

And so I do, _____ with - out a care. _

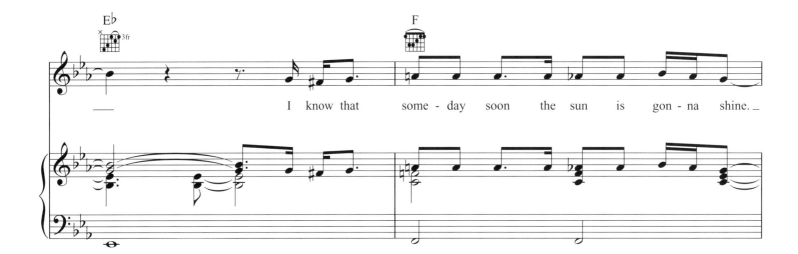

_ I know that some - day soon the sun is gon - na shine. _

_ And she'll be there, ____ this love of mine, _

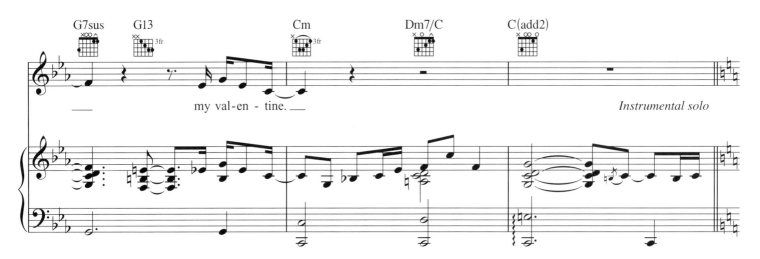

_ my val - en - tine. _

Instrumental solo

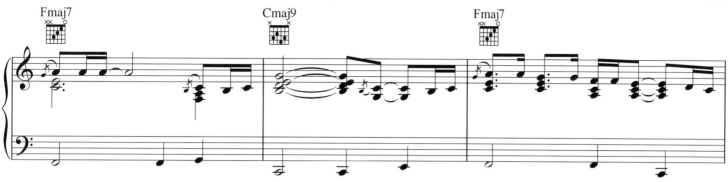

D.S. al Coda

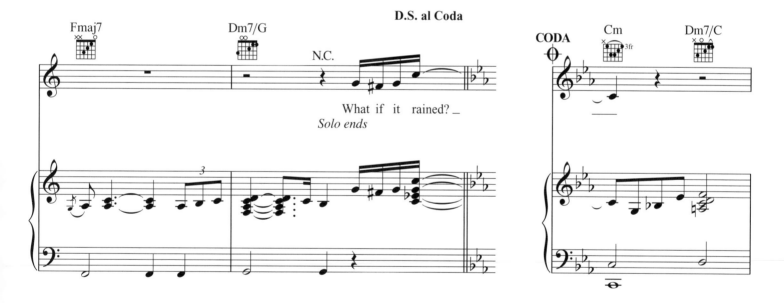

What if it rained? _
Solo ends

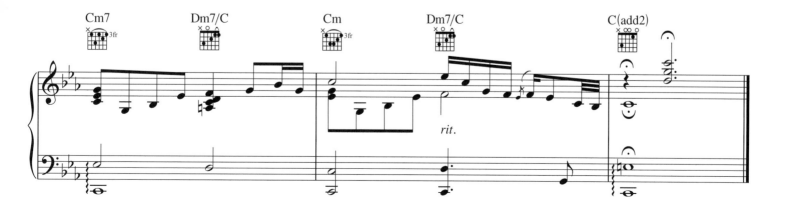

rit.

NINETEEN HUNDRED AND EIGHTY FIVE

Words and Music by
PAUL and LINDA McCARTNEY

Moderately fast

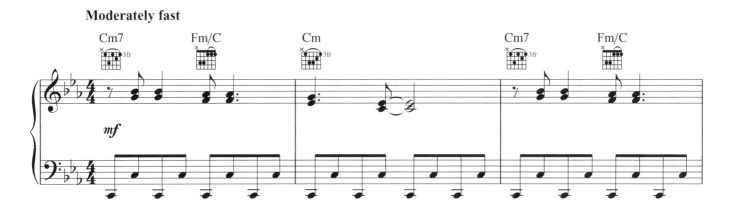

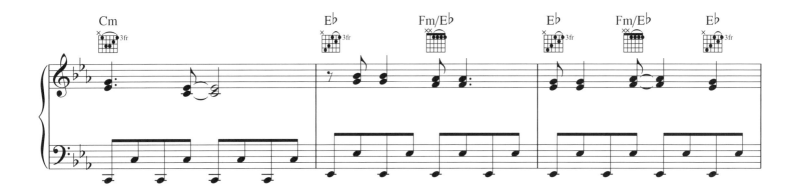

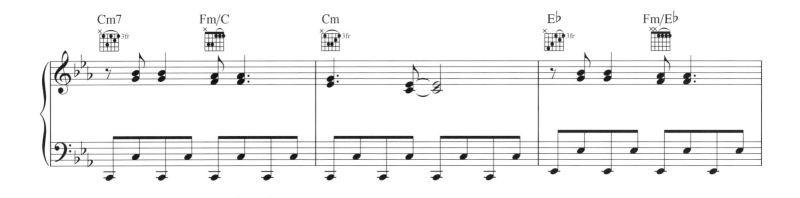

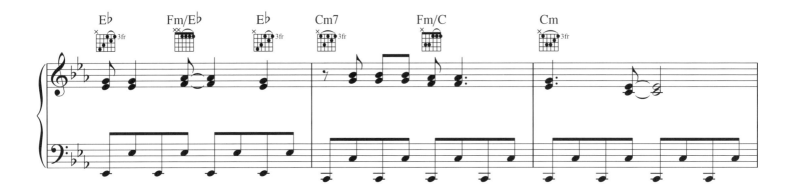

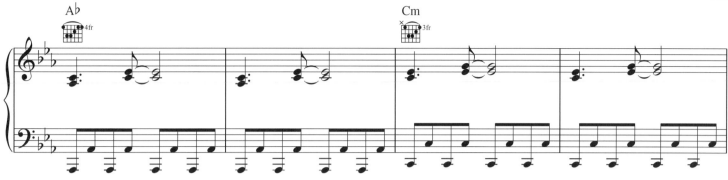

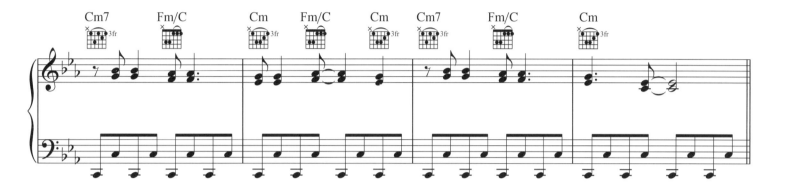

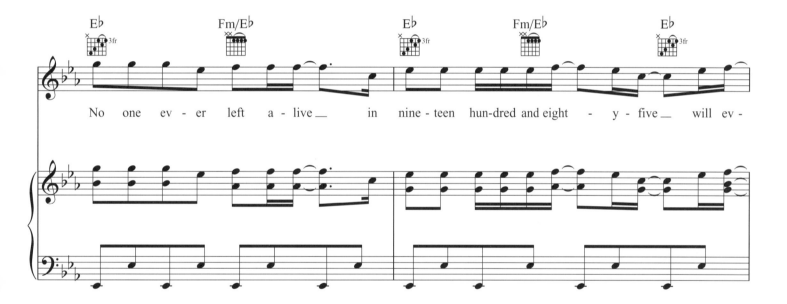

No one ev-er left a-live __ in nine-teen hun-dred and eight - y - five __ will ev-

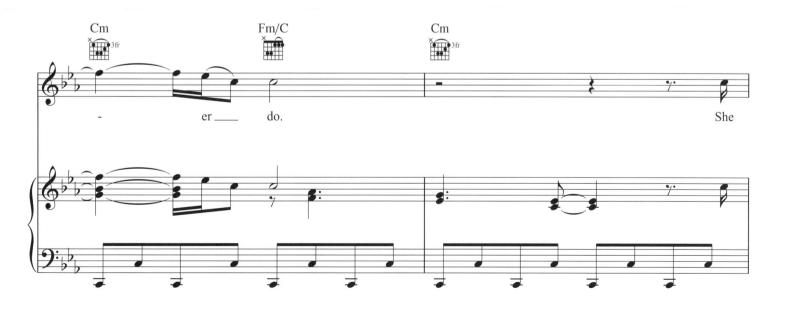

- er __ do.

She

stuff my lit-tle la - dy gets be-hind. ___

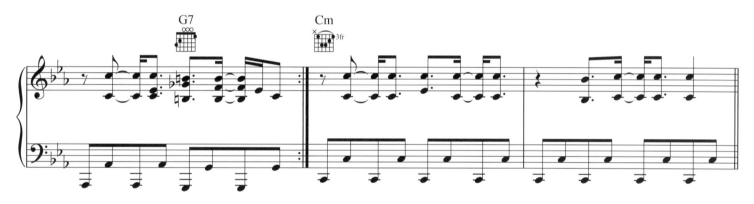

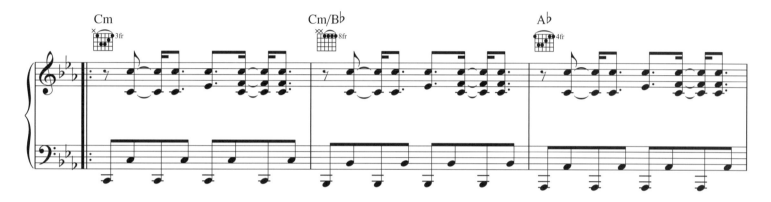

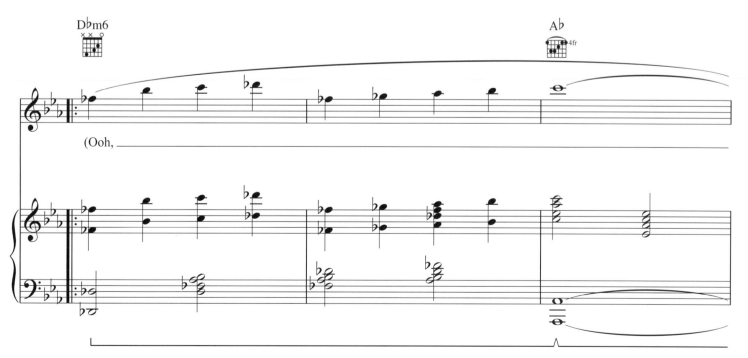

(Ooh, _____

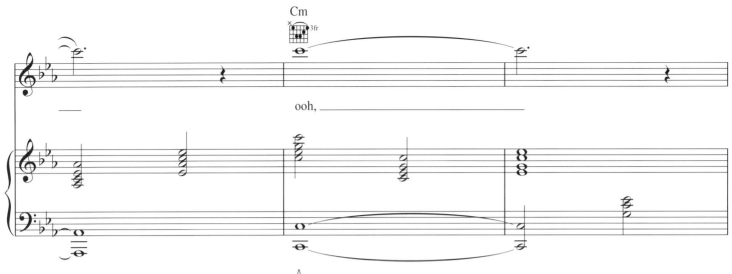

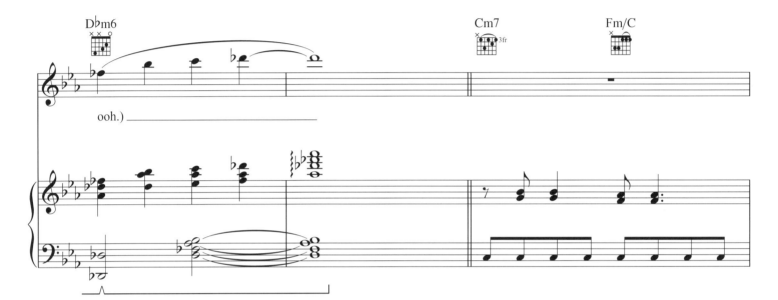

ooh,

ooh.)

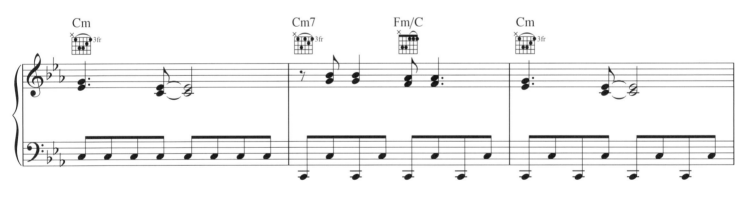

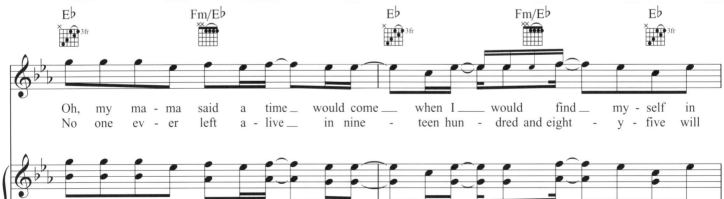

Oh, my ma - ma said a time_ would come_ when I_ would find_ my - self in
No one ev - er left a - live_ in nine - teen hun - dred and eight - y - five will

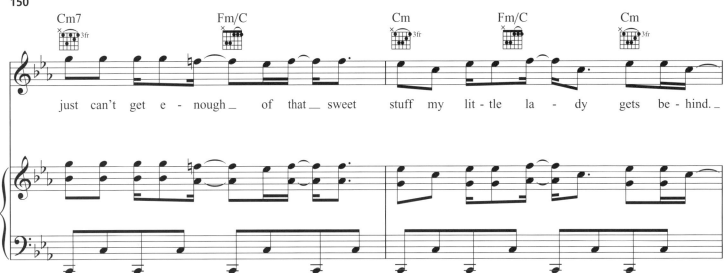

just can't get e - nough __ of that __ sweet stuff my lit - tle la - dy gets be - hind. __

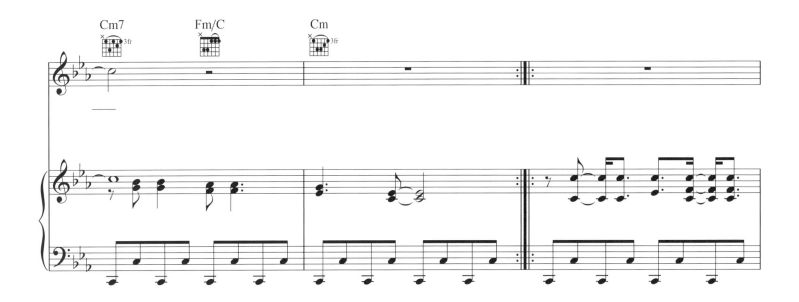

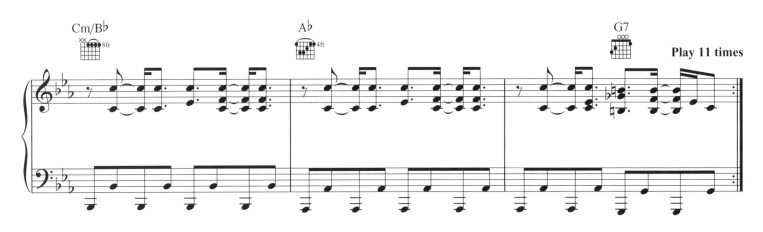

Play 11 times

SOMETHING

Words and Music by
GEORGE HARRISON

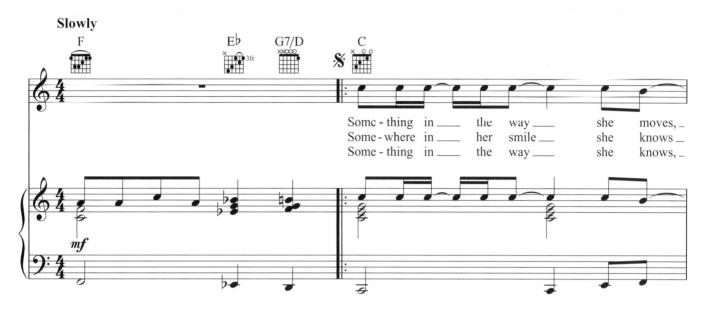

Something in ___ the way ___ she moves, ___
Some-where in ___ her smile ___ she knows, ___
Some-thing in ___ the way ___ she knows, ___

at-tracts ___ me like ___ no oth-er lov-er.
that I ___ don't need ___ no oth-er lov-er.
and all ___ I have ___ to do is think ___ of her.

Some-thing in ___ the way ___ she woos ___ me. ⎫
Some-thing in ___ her style ___ that shows ___ me. ⎬   I don't want to leave ___ her now,   you
Some-thing in ___ the things ___ she shows ___ me. ⎭

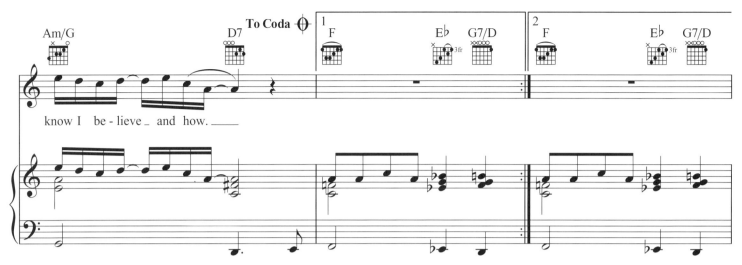

know I be - lieve _ and how. _____

You're ask-ing me _ will my _ love grow, I don't know, _

_____ I ____ don't know. You stick a - round _ now, it may

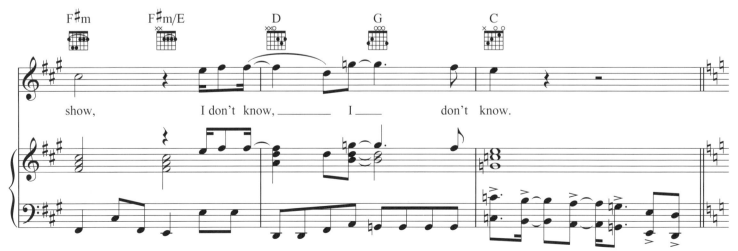

show, I don't know, _____ I ____ don't know.

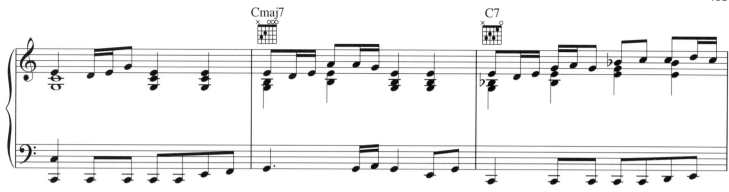

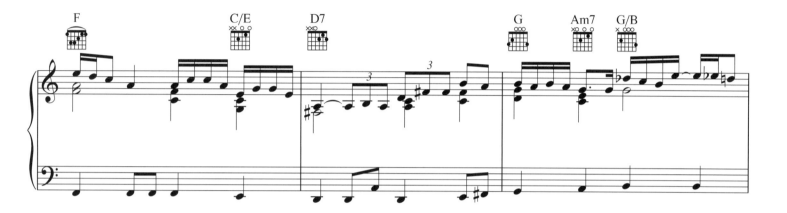

D.S. al Coda

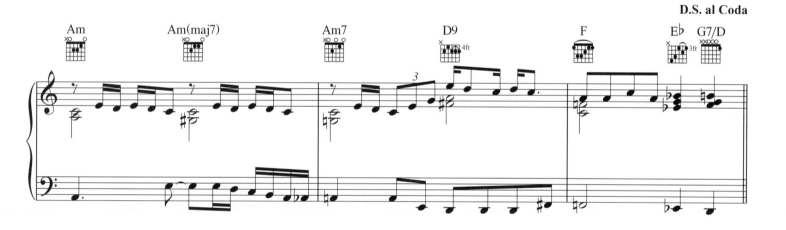

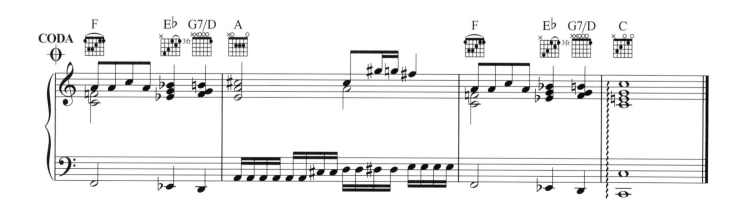

OB-LA-DI, OB-LA-DA

Words and Music by JOHN LENNON
and PAUL McCARTNEY

Des - mond has a bar - row in the
Des - mond takes a trol - ley to the

mar - ket place,____ Mol - ly is the sing - er in a
jewel - er's store,____ buys____ a twen - ty car - at gold - en

band. Des - mond says to Mol - ly, "Girl, I
ring. Takes____ it back to Mol - ly wait - ing

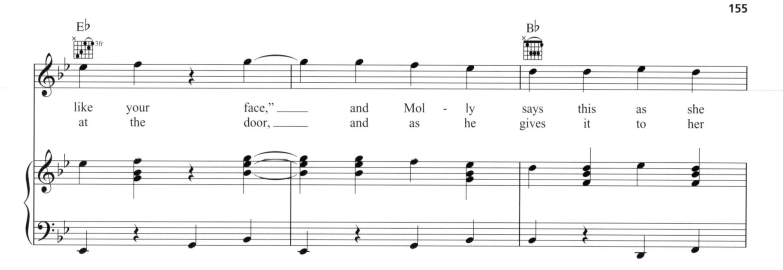

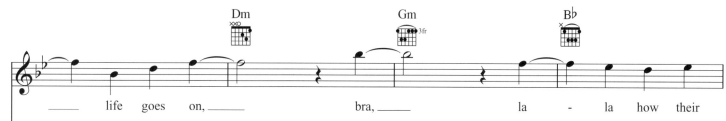

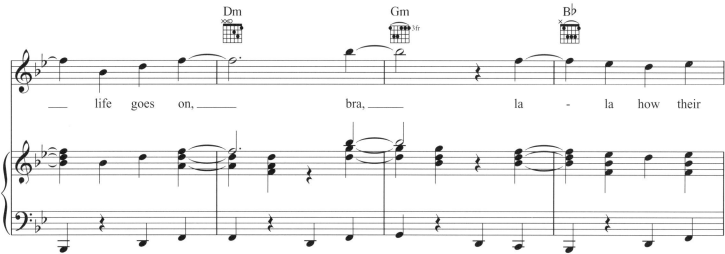

life goes on, ____ bra, ____ la - la how their

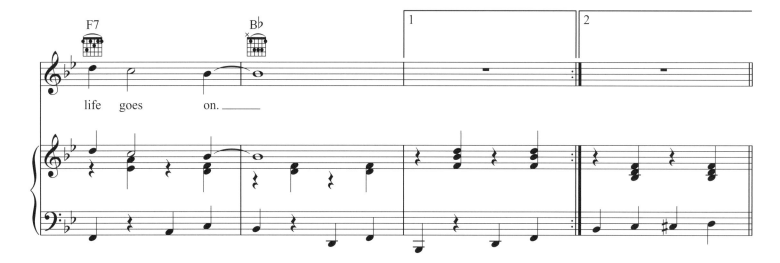

life goes on. ____

In a cou - ple of years, they have built a home ____ sweet home. ____

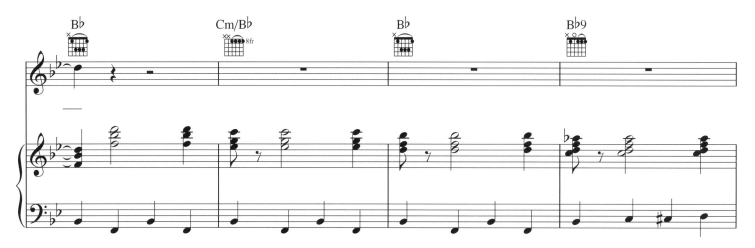

With a cou-ple of kids run - ning in the yard _____ of

Des - mond and Mol - ly Jones. _____

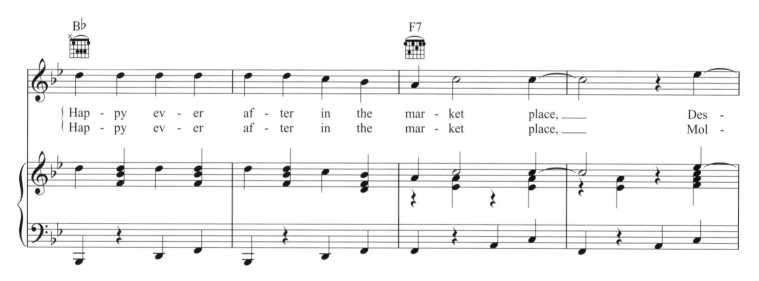

Hap - py ev - er af - ter in the mar - ket place, _____ Des -
Hap - py ev - er af - ter in the mar - ket place, _____ Mol -

- mond lets the chil - dren lend a hand. Mol -
- ly lets the chil - dren lend a hand. Des -

-ly stays at home and does her pret - ty face,____
-mond stays at home and does his pret - ty face,____

____ and in the eve - ning she still sings it with the band. ⎱
____ and in the eve - ning she's a sing - er with the band. ⎰

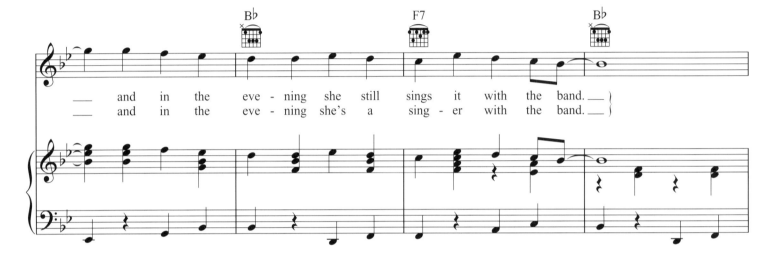

Ob - la - di,____ Ob - la - da,____ life goes on,____ bra,____

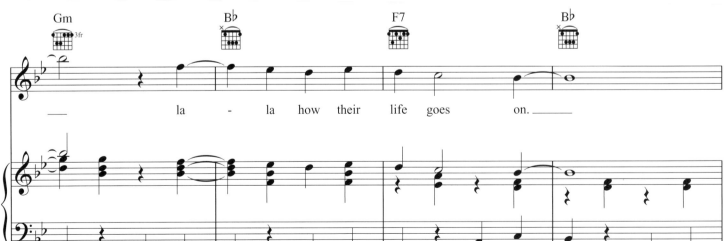

____ la - la how their life goes on.____

Ob - la - di, _____ Ob - la - da, _____ life goes on, _____ bra, __

__ la - la how their life goes on. _____

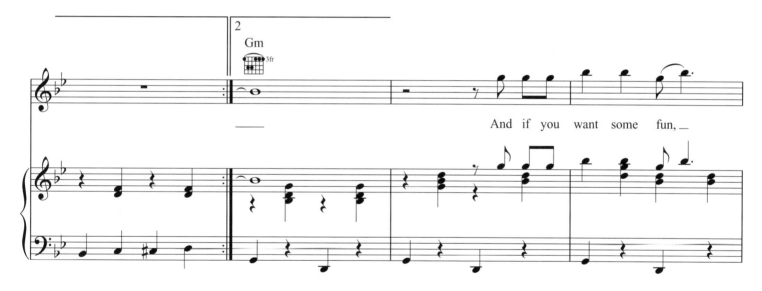

__ And if you want some fun, _

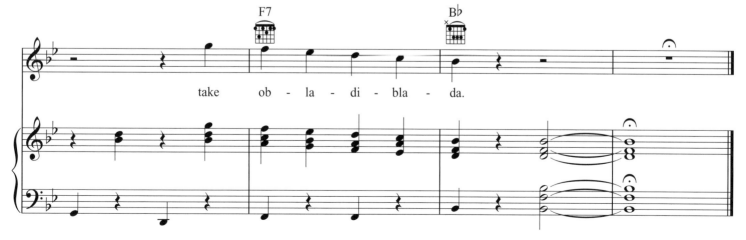

take ob - la - di - bla - da.

PAPERBACK WRITER

Words and Music by JOHN LENNON
and PAUL McCARTNEY

Bright Rock

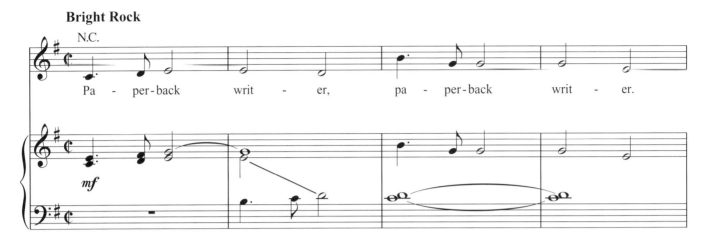

Pa - per-back writ - er, pa - per-back writ - er.

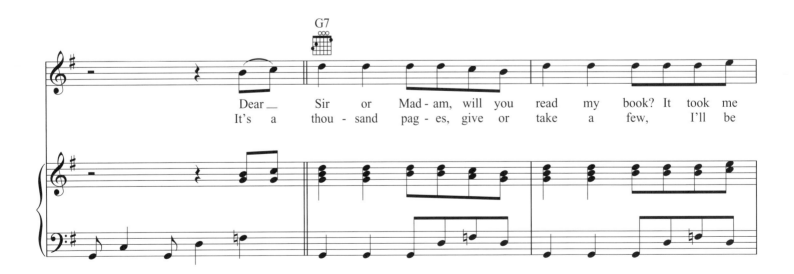

G7

Dear __ Sir or Mad - am, will you read my book? It took me
It's a thou - sand pag - es, give or take a few, I'll be

dirt - y man, ___ and his cling - ing wife ___ does - n't un - der - stand. His
have the rights, _ it could make a mil - lion for you o - ver - night. If you

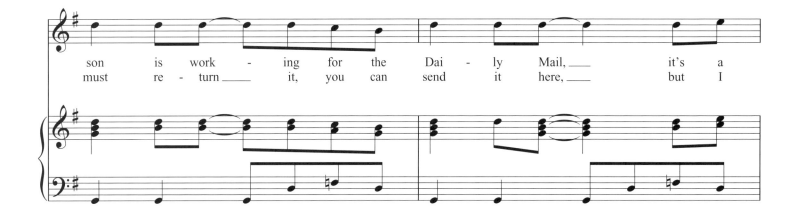

son is work - ing for the Dai - ly Mail, ___ it's a
must re - turn ___ it, you can send it here, ___ but I

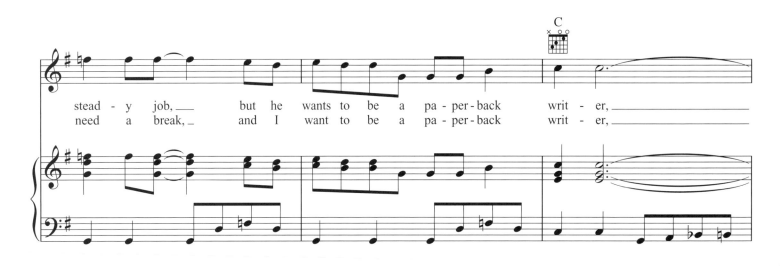

C

stead - y job, ___ but he wants to be a pa - per - back writ - er, ___
need a break, _ and I want to be a pa - per - back writ - er, ___

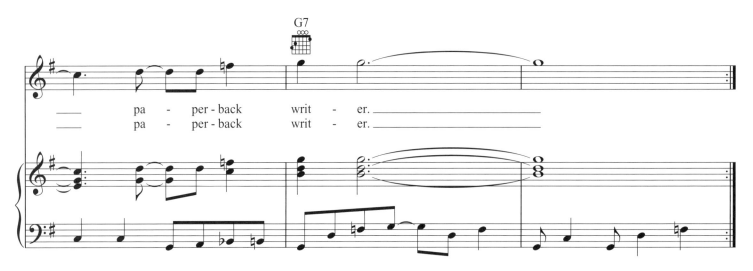

G7

___ pa - per - back writ - er. ___
___ pa - per - back writ - er. ___

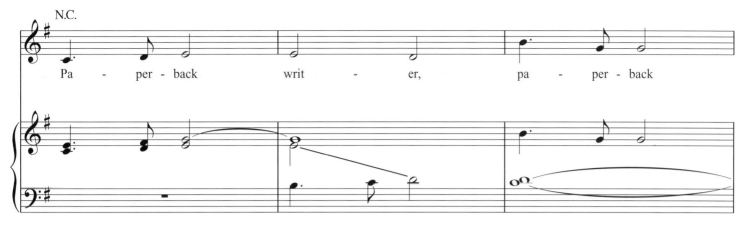

Repeat and Fade

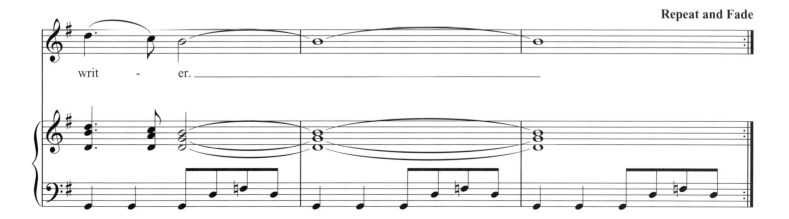

WE CAN WORK IT OUT

Words and Music by JOHN LENNON
and PAUL McCARTNEY

Try to see it my way, do I have to keep on talk-ing
Think of what you're say-ing, you can get it wrong and still you

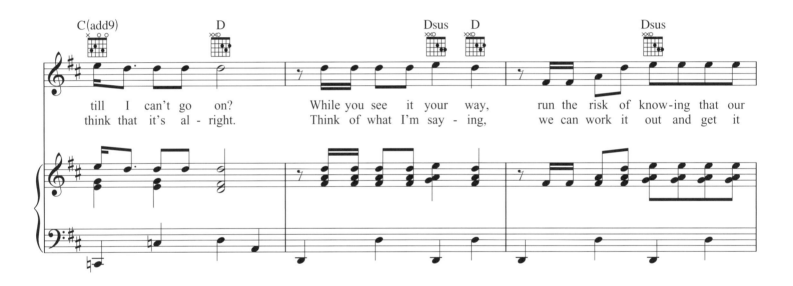

till I can't go on? While you see it your way, run the risk of know-ing that our
think that it's al-right. Think of what I'm say-ing, we can work it out and get it

love may soon be gone. } We can work it out, we can work it out. _____
straight, or say good-night. }

YESTERDAY

Words and Music by JOHN LENNON
and PAUL McCARTNEY

Moderately, with expression

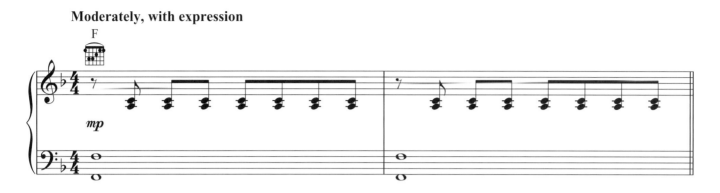

Yes - ter - day, _____ all my trou - bles seemed so
Sud - den - ly, _____ I'm not half the man I

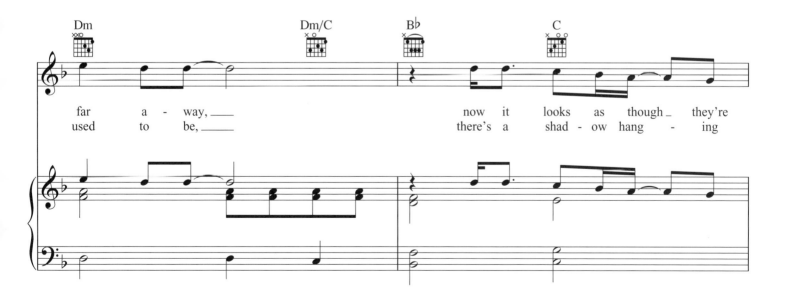

far a - way, _____ now it looks as though _ they're
used to be, _____ there's a shad - ow hang - ing

168

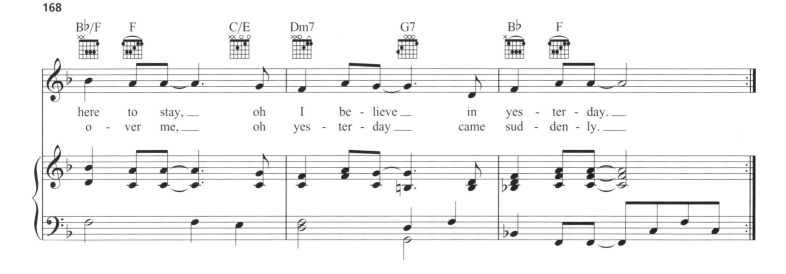

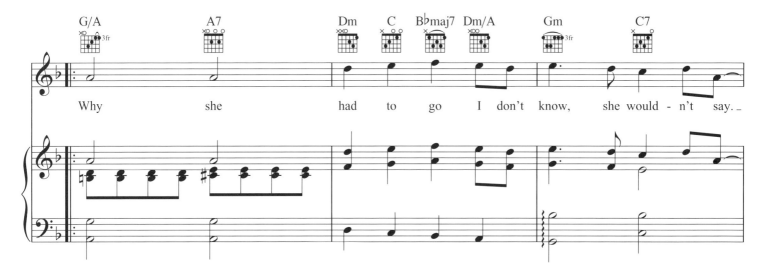

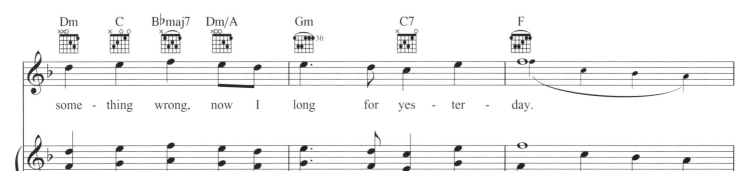

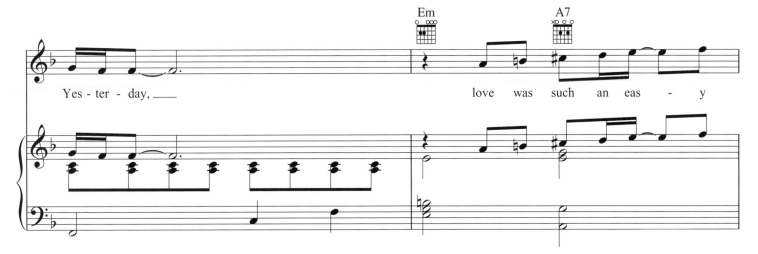

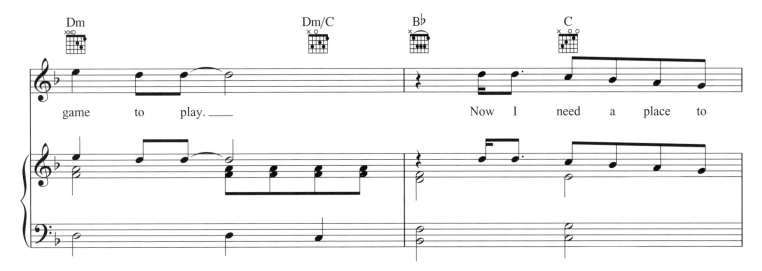

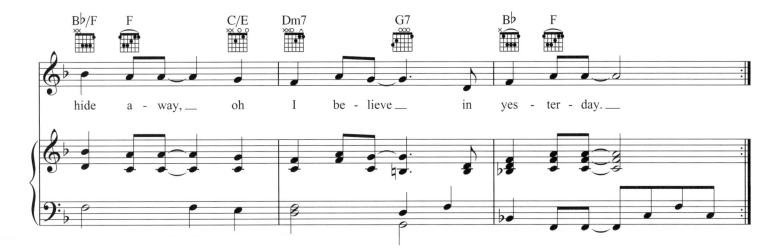

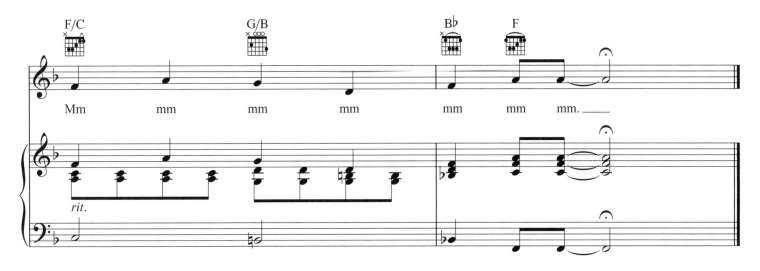

YOUR MOTHER SHOULD KNOW

Words and Music by JOHN LENNON
and PAUL McCARTNEY

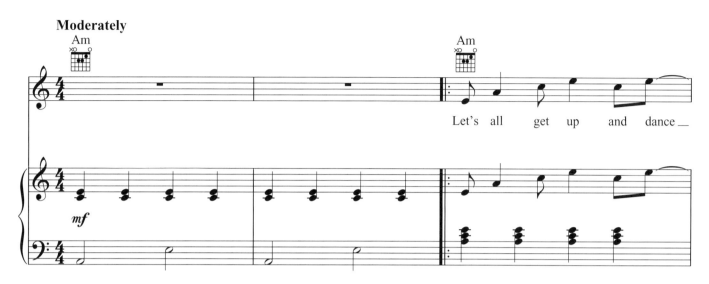

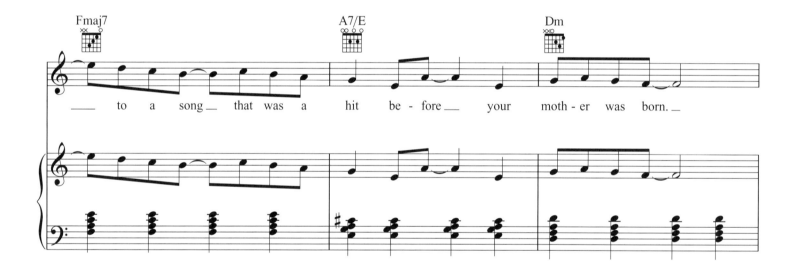

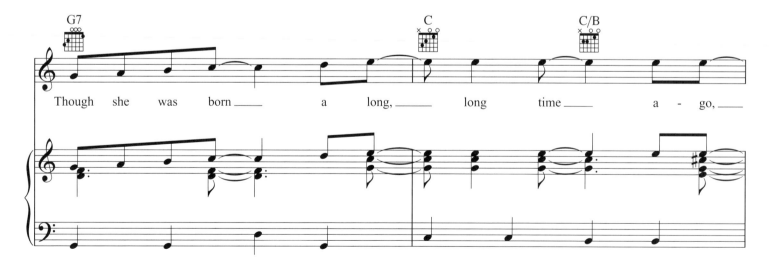

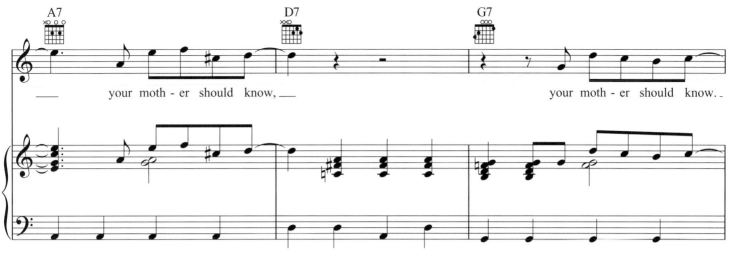

your moth - er should know, ___   your moth - er should know. ___

Sing it a - gain: ___

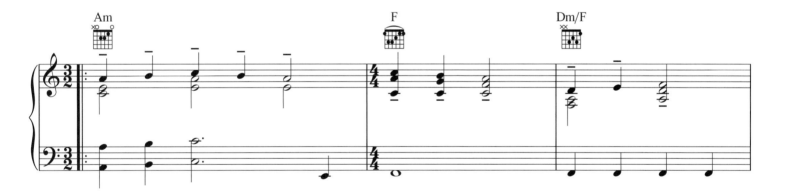

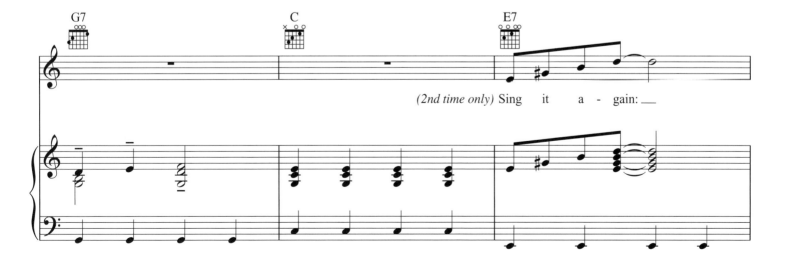

(2nd time only) Sing it a - gain: ___

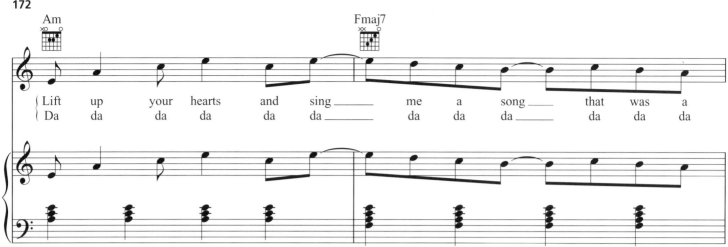

Lift up your hearts and sing ____ me a song ____ that was a
Da da da da da da da ____ da da da ____ da da da da

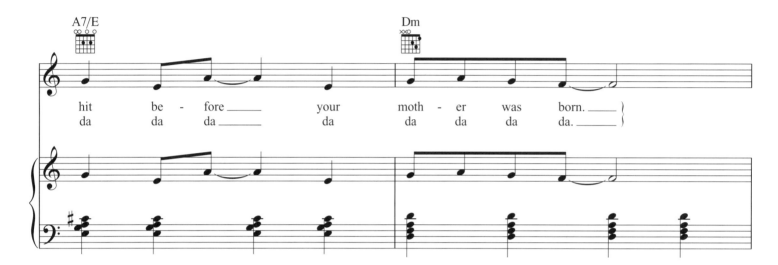

hit be - fore ____ your moth - er was born. ____
da da da ____ da da da da da born. ____

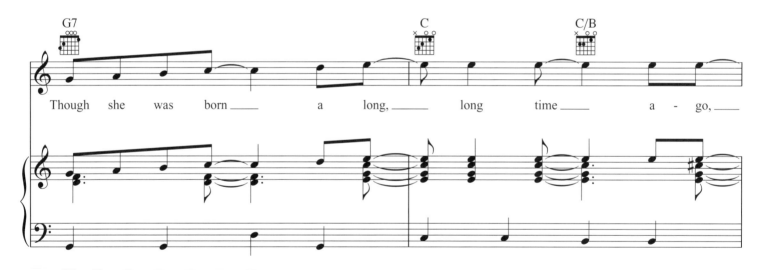

Though she was born ____ a long, ____ long time ____ a - go, ____

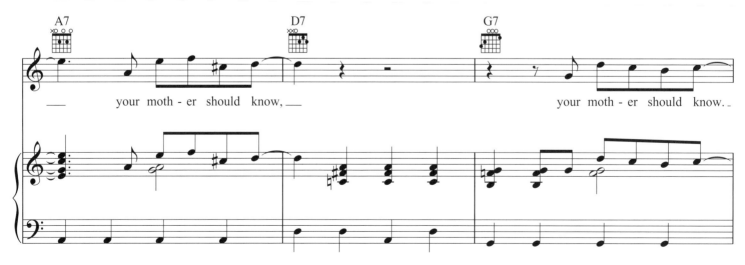

____ your moth - er should know, ____ your moth - er should know. ____